F

THE COMPLETE SPORTS MEDICINE BOOK FOR WOMEN

Mona Shangold, M.D.
Gabe Mirkin, M.D.

Produced by The Miller Press

FIRESIDE BOOKS
Published by Simon & Schuster, Inc.
New York

Copyright © 1985 by Mona Shangold, M.D. and Gabe Mirkin, M.D.

A Fireside Book,
published by Simon & Schuster, Inc.
Simon & Schuster Building
Rockefeller Center
1230 Avenue of the Americas
New York, New York 10020

FIRESIDE and colophon are registered trademarks of Simon &
Schuster, Inc.

Produced by The Miller Press, Incorporated.
Designed by Stanley S. Drate/Folio Graphics Co., Inc.

Manufactured in the United States of America

10 9 8 7 6 5 4 3 2 1

Library of Congress Cataloging in Publication Data

Shangold, Mona M.
    The complete sports medicine book for women.

    "A Fireside book."
    Includes index.
    1. Exercise for women. 2. Women—Health and hygiene.
3. Physical fitness for women. 4. Sports medicine.
I. Mirkin, Gabe. II. Title.
RA781.S52   1985   613.7′1′088042   84-21202
ISBN: 0-671-55722-X
ISBN: 0-671-53062-3 Pbk.

To our parents,
Vera and Mitchel Mirkin
and
Harriet and Jack Shangold,

our sister,
Naomi Mirkin Snyder,

and

our brothers,
Barry Mirkin
and
Gary Shangold,

who have inspired and helped us and who have always been there
when we needed them.

CONTENTS

FOREWORD

We have written this book to inform women about how exercise affects their bodies, how to deal with many problems that may arise in an exercise program, and how to prevent many of those problems too. Most women who attended school several decades ago were socially programmed to avoid exercise because it was considered "unfeminine." This avoidance later penalized many women with medical problems that are associated with a sedentary lifestyle and obesity, such as heart disease, gallbladder disease, diabetes, and certain cancers. We firmly believe that all women should exercise regularly, even if they have medical problems or other disabilities. From our unique combined perspectives as specialists in sports medicine, fitness, and women's health, we want to help all women receive the benefits of regular exercise and avoid the potential miseries.

It's harder for women over age 50 to acquire the motivation to engage in athletic activities, and they often feel some embarrassment when they do so because they were socially and culturally taught to avoid exertion. We hope this book will inspire and encourage many older women to exercise, for exercise is especially essential to these women.

It's much easier to maintain the habit of regular exercise throughout life, even into older age, if you have acquired the practice in youth. For this reason, we feel that young girls must learn to exercise because it is fun. Those who participate in sports to fulfill their parents' dreams usually abandon the habit before adulthood and remain sedentary thereafter.

We hope this book confirms your suspicions that it is both desirable and enjoyable to be fit. If you aren't already exercising regularly, we hope this book will encourage you to do so. If you already engage in physical activity on a regular basis, we hope this book will answer your questions about how exercise is affecting your body, how to enhance the benefits, how to reach your goals, and how to avoid exercise-related problems.

Mona Shangold, M.D.
Gabe Mirkin, M.D.

THE
COMPLETE
SPORTS
MEDICINE
BOOK
FOR
WOMEN

1 FINDING THE RIGHT EXERCISE PROGRAM

Everyone should exercise, but there are many different reasons why. Only you can decide what your personal goals are, and your unique set of aims will determine the best exercise program for you—which sports, how frequently, how vigorously, how long. Among the many goals which you can choose are a stronger heart, longer endurance, a faster pace, successful competition, stronger muscles, stronger bones, a thinner body, greater flexibility, better coordination, clearer thinking, and happier moods. Aim for any one or any combination of these. You may be surprised to find yourself achieving more goals than you have selected.

GOAL: STRONGER HEART

To strengthen your heart, you must exercise continuously in a sport that raises your heart rate to at least 120 beats per minute and keeps it that high for at least 10 minutes at a time, repeating this at least twice each week. You will benefit more if you sustain the exertion longer and repeat it more often. While you get greater benefits prolonging each session toward about 30 minutes, less improvement results from each increment after 30 minutes than from each increment up to 30 minutes. This means that you can strengthen your heart more if you exercise 30 minutes each time, rather than 10 minutes each time, but the rate of improvement slows down as you prolong each exercise session beyond 30 minutes. Similarly, you can strengthen your heart

Personal Goals (11 Reasons Why You Should Exercise)

1. Stronger heart
2. Longer endurance
3. Faster pace
4. Successful competition
5. Stronger muscles
6. Stronger bones
7. Thinner body
8. Greater flexibility
9. Better coordination
10. Clearer thinking
11. Happier moods

more by exercising three times each week rather than only twice, but the rate of improvement slows down as you exercise more than three times each week.

The sustained target rate of at least 120 beats per minute is important, but this number is merely an approximation, derived from scientific studies. To strengthen your heart, you must reach a heart rate equal to the sum of your resting heart rate and half of the difference between your maximum and resting heart rates. This difference is called your *heart rate reserve*. For most people, the maximum heart rate is equal to approximately 220 minus the age. So if you're 40 years old, your maximum heart rate is about 180. If your resting heart rate (taken with a finger on your pulse while you're lying in bed, preferably as soon as you awaken in the morning) is 60, your heart rate reserve is 120 (180 minus 60); half of 120 is 60; and your target heart rate is 120 (60 plus 60). Thus, you should exercise vigorously enough to keep your heart rate at 120 beats per minute or more, for at least 10 continuous minutes in each session, in order to strengthen your heart. For most people, regardless of age, the magic figure turns out to be around 120.

The type of exercise that leads to a sustained elevation of your heart rate is called *endurance exercise* or *aerobic exercise*. Sports that are included in this category are running, brisk walking, stationary bicycling, swimming, aerobic dancing, and cross-country skiing. Any activity qualifies if it is continuous and is carried out at a level supplying an adequate or nearly adequate amount of oxygen to do the work.

The rules for exercising to strengthen your heart are the same for women and men. Endurance training causes enlargement of the

How to Calculate Your Target Heart Rate

1. Subtract: 220 − age = maximum heart rate.
2. Count resting heart rate (while lying in bed).
3. Subtract: maximum heart rate − resting heart rate = heart rate reserve.
4. Divide: heart rate reserve divided by 2 = ½ heart rate reserve.
5. Add: resting heart rate + ½ heart rate reserve = target heart rate.

Example: If your age is 30 and your resting heart rate is 72:
1. *Subtract: 220 − 30 = 190.*
2. *Count resting heart rate = 72.*
3. *Subtract: 190 − 72 = 118.*
4. *Divide: 118 ÷ 2 = 59.*
5. *Add: 72 + 59 = 131.*

heart and strengthening of the heart muscle, and these effects occur in both men and women. While the average man has a slightly larger heart than the average woman, this may be due to the greater fitness of the average man, although there are no studies to prove or disprove this.

Definition of Cardiac Fitness

Strengthening your heart will enable you to achieve *cardiovascular fitness.* You are fit when your heart rate drops at least 30 beats per minute during the first 60 seconds after a maximum effort lasting at least five minutes. This decrement is called the *recovery pulse rate.* In order to calculate the decline precisely, you must measure your pulse during only the first five seconds after stopping the exercise, multiply this figure by 12, measure your pulse during a five-second interval after one minute has passed, multiply this figure by 12, and subtract the second number from the first. You can't determine your instantaneous heart rate at the conclusion of exercise by counting for an entire minute, since your heart rate will be much slower at the end of that

How to Calculate Your Recovery Pulse Rate

1. Exercise as hard as you can for at least five continuous minutes.
2. Count your pulse during the first five seconds after stopping the exercise.
3. Multiply this number by 12 = maximum pulse rate.
4. Allow exactly 60 seconds to pass.
5. Count your pulse during the next five seconds.
6. Multiply this number by 12 = pulse rate one minute later.
7. Subtract: maximum pulse rate − pulse rate one minute later = recovery pulse rate.

Example:
1. *Exercise as hard as you can for at least five continuous minutes.*
2. *Count your pulse during the first five seconds after stopping the exercise. (Suppose this is 15.)*
3. *Multiply this number by 12 = 180.*
4. *Allow exactly 60 seconds to pass.*
5. *Count your pulse during the next five seconds. (Suppose this is 11.)*
6. *Multiply this number by 12 = 132.*
7. *Subtract: 180 − 132 = 48.*

CAUTION: This test can injure an already damaged heart. Do not do this test if there is any chance that your heart is not normal.

minute than it was at the start. That is why you have to multiply the number of beats in the first five seconds by 12 and the number in the last five seconds by 12. (There are 12 five-second intervals in each minute.)

As you become more fit, your heart rate will return toward normal sooner after you've finished exercising. This happens because your muscles will have increased amounts of enzymes which enable them to remove lactic acid, the breakdown product resulting from an oxygen deficit. As you become more fit, you should be able to exercise at any level more easily and can exercise at higher levels than you could before.

Maximum Oxygen Uptake

Your *oxygen uptake* is the amount of oxygen your body uses to perform any given amount of work. Greater work loads require more oxygen. Your *maximum oxygen uptake* is the maximum amount of oxygen that can be taken in by your body, delivered to your muscles, and used by them. This value is a measure of how fit you are. As you become more fit, this level will rise. You can undergo a special test in an exercise physiology laboratory to determine your maximum oxygen uptake. In this test, you will run on a treadmill or pedal on a stationary bicycle as vigorously as possible, inhaling and exhaling air that has had its oxygen content measured.

Your maximum oxygen uptake correlates roughly with the pace at which you can exercise comfortably. As a general rule, faster runners have higher levels of maximum oxygen uptake. Of course, heavier people perform more work than lighter people, when both exercise at the same pace. Therefore, it is probably fairest to include your weight in any calculations of your maximum oxygen uptake, since you're really doing more work if you exercise while carrying more weight. Because you can't leave your fat at the starting line of any race, it's not surprising that the front-runners are usually very thin, since they have little excess fat to carry with them. Your work load at any pace depends mostly upon the total weight of your body, which you must carry with you. This is especially true in activities like running. The work incurred during stationary bicycling is less dependent upon body weight because much of your weight can just sit on the seat, while your legs move up and down to pedal. The work incurred during swimming, too, is less dependent upon body weight, since the water buoys you up and makes you weigh less than you would on land.

Anaerobic Threshold

Your *anaerobic threshold* is that level of exercise above which you begin to accumulate significant amounts of lactic acid in your bloodstream. Lactic acid accumulates whenever too little oxygen is provided to your muscles to meet their needs, to enable them to do the work they're doing. Since regular training teaches your body to deliver more oxygen to your muscles, your anaerobic threshold rises with conditioning. This means that you will be able to work harder before you begin to incur an oxygen debt, delaying the point at which you will begin to accumulate lactic acid.

GOAL: LONGER ENDURANCE

In order to run, bicycle, or swim for a longer time, you must store more sugar as a source of energy in your muscles. Sugar is stored in your muscles in the form of glycogen. The more glycogen you can store in your muscles, the longer you can exercise them. To store more glycogen in your muscles, you must incorporate a weekly *depletion workout* into your training program. This entails exercising in your chosen sport until you have depleted the glycogen in your muscles. They will refill when you eat carbohydrate-rich food afterward, and they will fill with more glycogen than they contained before. If you are a highly trained athlete, it will take at least 1½ to 2 hours of continuous running to accomplish such a depletion, or 4 to 6 hours of continuous bicycling, or 10 to 12 hours of cross-country skiing. Of course, if you are in poor shape, it will take even less time to deplete your muscles. Training is specific: Long training workouts are necessary if you want to prepare for long competitive events. Athletes in most sports deplete their muscles once a week. Doing a depletion workout more often than once a week may lead to injuries and impaired performance. Depleting less often than once every two weeks is probably not effective in maintaining endurance.

Depletion rules are the same for both men and women. Back in the days when women were discouraged from doing any activities that led to sweating and aching, depletion was uncommon among women. Long, sustained exercise is safe for healthy men and women, and such exercise is necessary for prolonging endurance.

GOAL: FASTER PACE

In order to run, bicycle, or swim at a faster pace, you must teach your muscles to move faster, tolerate the discomfort of lactic acid accumulation, and remove the lactic acid faster too. You can accomplish this by (1) exercising continuously at a very fast pace or (2) doing very short intervals at a very fast pace interspersed with recovery periods in which you exercise for a short time at a very leisurely pace. *Interval training* refers to doing a fixed number of repetitions over a fixed distance at a fixed pace with a fixed recovery. (The *recovery* is the slowly exercised distance after each fast burst.) For example, you may run 10 quarter-miles in 100 seconds each, separated by a slow jog of an eighth of a mile between each fast run. If you want to get faster, you may want to include an interval workout in your program at least once, but not more than three times, each week.

Alternate Hard and Easy Days

You'll improve by doing intervals once or twice a week, but be sure you don't do them on consecutive days. Every time you exercise vigorously, your muscles are injured slightly, and it takes 48 hours for them to recover. It's a good idea to exercise lightly on the easy day, rather than resting altogether. You may even prefer to switch to another sport for the easy workout. Always listen to your body, in order to avoid overuse injuries. (See Chapter 5.) If your body feels tight after a recent vigorous workout, you may prefer to take the day off altogether.

Long and Short Intervals

Long intervals are fast laps that last at least two minutes each; these teach you to tolerate the discomfort that accompanies a high level of lactic acid, and also teach your body to eliminate lactic acid faster. The high levels of lactic acid in your bloodstream tire you quickly, so that even great athletes don't do more than four or six of these long intervals in any average workout.

Short intervals are fast laps that last a maximum of 30 seconds each; these teach your brain to coordinate your muscles at a faster pace. Both long and short intervals are performed almost as fast as you can. Since very little lactic acid accumulates during each short interval, you'll be able to accomplish a lot more short intervals than long intervals in any workout. Top athletes do as many as a hundred repetitions of short intervals in a workout.

GOAL: SUCCESSFUL COMPETITION

If you want to compete, interval training is an excellent type of training. Many women who went to school several decades ago lacked the encouragement to become competitive. Casual, recreational exercise was the most they aimed for, even if they were born with a great amount of natural athletic ability. You may be one of

Sample Running Program For Improving Speed and Endurance

FOR THE MIDDLE-OF-THE-ROAD RUNNER

SUNDAY:

Long run lasting one hour, done at a pace that is faster than the pace of your easier days.

MONDAY:

Slow, comfortable run* lasting 30 to 60 minutes.

TUESDAY:

A three-mile run at a fast pace.

WEDNESDAY:

Slow, comfortable run* lasting 30 to 60 minutes.

THURSDAY:

A 7 to 10 mile run at a fast pace.

FRIDAY:

Slow, comfortable run* lasting 30 to 60 minutes.

SATURDAY:

Take the day off or jog 30 to 60 minutes at a comfortable pace.

FOR THE SERIOUS, DEDICATED RUNNER

SUNDAY:

Long run lasting at least two hours, done at comfortable pace.

MONDAY:

Slow, comfortable run* lasting 30 to 60 minutes.

TUESDAY:

Short-interval workout: One hundred 110-yard bursts at top speed (each in 20 seconds or less, if possible), separated by the same distance at slow pace.

WEDNESDAY:

    Slow, comfortable run* lasting 30 to 60 minutes.

THURSDAY:

    Long-interval workout: Six 880-yard bursts at near-top speed (each in three minutes or less, depending on level of fitness), separated by the same distance at slow place.

FRIDAY:

    Slow, comfortable run* lasting 30 to 60 minutes.

SATURDAY:

    Slow, comfortable run* lasting 30 to 60 minutes.

*Swimming or bicycling may be substituted for one or two of these runs.

these women, and this may be the right time for you to become a competitive athlete. However, no one can select this goal for you. If you have no desire to compete, you don't need to do speed work, and it's perfectly all right to exercise slowly all the time. Never feel uncomfortable or embarrassed to exercise at your own chosen pace.

On the other hand, many women who were programmed to believe that strenuous exercise was "unfeminine" actually have a good deal of ability. What some of them lack is motivation and confidence. Such women deserve as much encouragement and support as possible, in order to enable them to train properly to develop their skills and meet their goals.

GOAL: STRONGER MUSCLES

If you want to strengthen any muscle, you must contract the muscle against resistance. Exercising without resistance does not give you strong muscles. If it did, long-distance runners would be stronger than weight lifters, who spend far fewer hours exercising. Obviously, weight lifters are much stronger.

Each muscle is made up of thousands of stringlike fibers. When you contract any muscle against resistance (for example, lifting a heavy weight or pushing on a strength-training machine), you actually use only a small percentage of the total number of fibers in the entire muscle. Each successive contraction with the same weight recruits additional muscle fibers until the muscle becomes acidic from the accumulation of lactic acid. When this happens, the number of fibers contracting will decrease and so will the training benefit. Continuing to lift weights after this fatigue point has been reached may lead to injuries, as well. It takes 30 to 50 seconds of heavy lifting for muscles to accumulate large amounts of lactic acid. You can lift a heavy weight slowly 8 to 12 times in 30 to 50 seconds. So, if you want to become strong, you should pick the heaviest weight that you can lift comfortably 8 consecutive times. Do this every other day. As you become stronger, you will be able to lift that same weight 9, 10, 11, and then 12 times. When you can lift the weight 12 consecutive times, add 5 to 10 pounds to your lift and reduce the number of consecutive lifts to 8 again.

Of course, you'll be able to do many more repetitions if you lift a lighter weight. However, you won't gain strength unless your muscles contract against resistance, and this requires a relatively heavy weight. Lifting light weights for many repetitions lasting for at least 10 consecutive minutes can lead to aerobic improvement (strengthening your heart), but it won't strengthen the muscle significantly.

All women can benefit from lifting weights. Because women tend to have weak upper-body muscles, it is often difficult for them to perform many ordinary tasks such as carrying children, books, or groceries and opening heavy doors and tight jars. These particular tasks are part of day-to-day life for both men and women. However, these chores are usually done much more easily by men, who naturally have more upper-body strength. You will find it easier to do many of your daily tasks if your arms are stronger.

There are three types of muscle contractions: isotonic, isometric, and isokinetic. An *isotonic* contraction (also called *dynamic)* is one in which the muscle shortens as it develops tension. You do this type of contraction when you raise a barbell. An *isometric* contraction (also called *static)* is one in which the muscle develops tension but does not change its length. You do this type of contraction when you try to lift an immovable object or push against an immovable wall. An *isokinetic* contraction is one in which the muscle moves at a constant speed. Your arms do a motion that is almost an isokinetic contraction during freestyle swimming, and several specialized machines can permit you to do this also. Nautilus and Cybex equipment are examples of such machines.

Of these three types of muscle contractions, isometric training offers the greatest convenience and least expense, since no special equipment is required. Isokinetic training offers the lowest risk of injury. The machines control your movements, so you are far less likely to overextend a joint. Isotonic training is preferred by many athletes because they prefer to lift free weights.

However, each of the three types of muscle contractions has drawbacks. Isometric contractions make you strong only at the angle at which you hold a joint. For example, when you push against a wall with your elbows bent, you will become strong only within twenty degrees of the angle at which you hold your elbow. Isokinetic contractions usually require machines that are too expensive for the average person, so she will usually have to join an expensive club to use them. Isotonic contractions usually are done by lifting weights, and this requires a great amount of skill. Some of the worst injuries in strength training occur during free weight lifting.

Lifting weights is another activity that has traditionally been considered "unfeminine," and many woman avoided this practice because they feared they would develop large, unsightly muscles. This fear is totally unwarranted. Women can make their muscles much stronger without making them large and bulky. This is true because women have low levels of the masculinizing hormone *testosterone*, which is needed for significant muscle enlargement. Men naturally have much higher levels of this hormone than women do, and as a result men have a natural tendency to become muscular. As we discuss in Chapter 3, growth hormone also enlarges and strengthens muscles. However, it isn't certain whether adding testosterone or growth hormone to a normal body will enlarge and strengthen muscles, unless training is intensified too.

GOAL: STRONGER BONES

All people should strive to have thick, strong bones because such bones are less likely to break. Our bones have a natural tendency to get thinner and weaker as we get older, and several factors can accelerate this thinning process. If you are sedentary, if you smoke cigarettes, or if you consume inadequate dietary calcium, your bones will get thinner at an earlier age. Most adults need 1,000 milligrams of dietary calcium daily to maintain bone thickness. After the menopause, women require 1,500 milligrams of dietary calcium daily. (See Chapters 2 and 9.)

Exercised bones become thicker and stronger, as long as dietary calcium is adequate. Champion tennis players use one arm more than the other for several hours each day. The bones in the racquet arm are much thicker and stronger than those in the arm that does not hold the racquet.

Bone thinning *(osteoporosis)* is a serious health hazard for all aging people. Breaking a major bone can lead to many serious complications. The bed rest required for healing of major fractures increases a victim's chance of having an undesirable blood clot settle in the lungs, legs, or elsewhere. Everyone should be encouraged to exercise regularly to strengthen the bones, even people who lack dexterity and a competitive instinct.

GOAL: THINNER BODY

Women have a natural disadvantage in the quest for thinness. The feminizing hormone *estrogen* tends to promote the formation of fat, particularly in the breasts, thighs, and hips. Because normal women have much higher levels of this hormone than men do, women have a natural tendency to become fatter than men. The social programming that tends to discourage exercise in women tends to make this propensity even worse.

Obesity is a disease of underactivity rather than a disease of overeating. In fact, most thin people who are active eat more than most obese people who are inactive. Dr. Peter Wood of Stanford has shown that the average active thin person consumes 600 calories a day more than the average obese person. Because thin people tend to be active, they find it easier to remain thin; because fat people tend to be inactive, they find it difficult to lose fat.

If you lose weight quickly by dieting, the weight you lose will be mostly muscle. The best way to lose fat is by a combination of diet and exercise. Exercise promotes a loss of fat in several ways. First of all, sustained exertion (which occurs in all of the endurance sports that have been described, including running, brisk walking, stationary bicycling, swimming, aerobic dancing, and cross-country skiing) burns a lot of calories during the actual exercise session. In addition, endurance exercise also speeds up your metabolism, so you will burn more calories after you finish exercising.

Because muscle requires more energy to be maintained than fat, muscular people burn more calories than fat people of the same weight. Muscles contain protein, which is made up of building blocks called amino acids. (See Chapter 2.) The amino acids are constantly passing from the muscle into the bloodstream and then back into the muscle. It takes energy to move these amino acids into and out of the muscle. On the other hand, fat is inert, requiring very little energy to be maintained. The more active any tissue is, the more energy it requires for maintenance. This means that it uses up calories. If you exercise regularly enough to maintain reasonable muscle tone, you will burn more calories even while resting.

If you lose fat through an endurance exercise program, you will lose the fat from all over your body. Half of the fat in your body is located just underneath your skin and over your muscles. When you lose fat, some will be lost from the deposits which surround your muscles. As a result, you may be able to see muscles that you never noticed before. Some women mistakenly assume that their muscles have gotten larger, but the increased visibility of these muscles is really due to shedding of the fat layers covering these muscles.

Society has changed its opinion of obesity over the last 60 years. It was once fashionable to be fat. Now it is considered fashionable to be thin. Cleopatra was fat and Rubens never would have painted a thin woman. Most of the great artists have portrayed only plump women and muscular men. Fat women had more wealth and prestige; thin women became thin by working hard for survival, with little dietary excess. A sedentary lifestyle was associated with luxury, and this attitude produced many generations of fat women. Their muscles were covered by so much fat that the muscles couldn't be seen. However, standards of beauty have changed greatly. It is now undesirable and unattractive to be fat. The most attractive body a woman can have is one that reveals toned muscles and very little fat. Well-defined and shapely muscles are attractive on every woman.

GOAL: GREATER FLEXIBILITY

Your flexibility determines how far you can bend, and it depends on how far you can stretch your muscles without tearing them. Flexibility helps to prevent injuries by decreasing the tension on muscles. It can help to reduce muscle soreness and enhance certain types of athletic performance.

The best way to improve your flexibility is by slow, deliberate stretching. Rapid stretching can be dangerous and ineffective. *Ballistic stretching* involves quick, jerky, bouncing movements (for example, rapid toe touches). This type of stretching is dangerous because it often places too much tension on the muscle being stretched. It's often ineffective because it activates the involuntary *stretch reflex*, which contracts the muscle you're trying to relax. *Passive stretching* involves stretching a muscle group by using an external force to do the work (for example, having a friend push your bent knees toward your shoulders while you're lying on your back, to passively stretch your hamstrings). Although this type of stretching can improve your flexibility, you must be careful to avoid overstretching by the outside force. *Static stretching* involves a slow, deliberate stretch until you feel a tightness in the muscle (but stopping before you feel pain). Hold this slow stretch for at least 30 seconds, in order to achieve relaxation of the muscle. (You usually can't tell that relaxation is taking place.) This type of stretch is safest and is very effective in promoting flexibility. Stretching beyond the point at which you feel pain is dangerous and may tear your muscle fibers. Such an injury will set you back in your training because you will have to wait until the muscle heals before you can stretch it again safely.

It's safest and wisest to stretch your muscles when they're warm. This is why you should exercise your muscles to warm them up before you stretch them. Warm muscles are less likely than cold muscles to tear during exercise, and warm muscles that have been stretched are even less likely to tear during vigorous exercise. This greater extensibility lasts for approximately three hours after stretching. So it's advisable to warm up and then stretch before a competitive event or any other vigorous workout.

Stretching before a vigorous workout reduces your chances of being injured, and stretching after a hard workout enhances your muscle relaxation and reduces your muscle soreness. After any vigorous exercise, your muscles are injured slightly, and they shorten slightly as they heal. If you exercise regularly, your muscles will gradually tighten with time, limiting your flexibility and increasing your chances of injuring your muscles. Thus, regular exercisers in any sport should stretch after or during every workout, to maintain flexibility and comfort.

Women are still more likely than men to injure themselves while exercising. This inequality is due to poor conditioning among average women. Long ago, women never learned how to train properly. Schoolgirls exercised infrequently and without preparation. The injuries that resulted were attributed to inherent sexual differences. In fact, the injury difference resulted from different teaching and different practice. Men were taught to get in shape *before* exercising, and women were taught to get in shape *by* exercising.

Women *are* as well suited as men to all types of exercise. To help them to avoid soreness and injury, both men and women should keep their muscles loose and relaxed by stretching. Warm your muscles before you stretch them, by exercising slowly in the same way you will be using them. For example, warm up for running by jogging slowly, warm up for tennis by hitting several practice shots, and warm up for ice hockey by skating slowly.

Warming up and stretching are very different aspects of conditioning. When you *warm up,* you raise the temperature of your muscles by generating heat in them as they are exercised. This warming enables your muscles to contract more forcefully and with less chance of injury. Stretching a warm muscle before exercise enhances these effects; stretching a warm muscle after exercise may reduce subsequent soreness and tightness. Stretching a cold muscle (before exercise) is often dangerous and painful.

Cooling down is the process by which you continue moving for a few minutes after you have completed your workout. Continued activity at this time keeps your blood circulating faster than it would have circulated if you had stood, sat, or lain still. This increased circulation delivers more blood to your skin, which eliminates the heat and cools you off. This circulation also decreases your chances of passing out from an irregular heartbeat or from an inadequate supply of blood reaching your heart. When you exercise, your leg muscles serve as a second heart to pump blood back to your heart. When your leg muscles relax, the veins near them fill up with blood. When your leg muscles contract, they squeeze against the veins and force the blood up toward the heart.

In summary, before each workout, you should warm up and then stretch your warm muscles. After each workout, you should cool down and then stretch again.

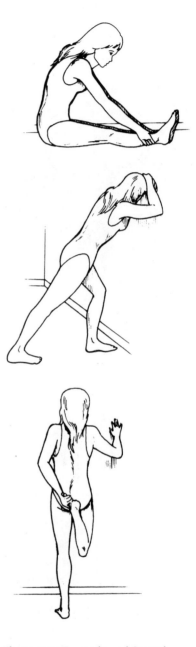

Figure 1-1. Examples of Stretching Exercises. In each exercise, stretch as far as you can comfortably stretch and hold the stretch for at least 30 seconds.

Sample Balanced Exercise Program for Fitness and Health

SUNDAY:

Slow, comfortable run lasting 30 minutes; upper-body weight lifting lasting 15 minutes; static stretching for 15 minutes, using both upper- and lower-body muscle groups.

MONDAY:

Aerobic dancing lasting 30 minutes; static stretching for 15 minutes, using both upper- and lower-body muscle groups.

TUESDAY:

Steady stationary bicycling for 30 minutes; upper-body weight lifting lasting 15 minutes; static stretching for 15 minutes, using both upper- and lower-body muscle groups.

WEDNESDAY:

Slow, comfortable swim lasting 30 minutes; static stretching for 15 minutes, using both upper- and lower-body muscle groups.

THURSDAY:

Slow, comfortable run lasting 30 minutes; upper-body weight lifting lasting 15 minutes; static stretching for 15 minutes, using both upper- and lower-body muscle groups.

FRIDAY:

Aerobic dancing lasting 30 minutes; static stretching for 15 minutes, using both upper- and lower-body muscle groups.

SATURDAY:

Steady stationary bicycling for 30 minutes; static stretching for 15 minutes, using both upper- and lower-body muscle groups. Or, it is perfectly all right for you to take the day off.

GOAL: BETTER COORDINATION

Coordination is partly inherited and partly cultivated. Although you can't select different parents, you can still improve the dexterity with which you were born. To move any part of your body, you must teach your brain to contract and relax the appropriate muscles. Your brain sends a signal along specific nerves to the muscles they control. The more your brain practices sending any signal, the better it can send the signal and orchestrate the task.

To fire a tennis serve into the appropriate spot on the court, you must practice the task repeatedly, teaching your brain to coordinate your muscles precisely. If you want to score free throws or layup shots on the basketball court, you must practice these specific maneuvers also.

The same rule for developing coordination applies to men and women: PRACTICE. Although some people are born with more skill than others, there are no sexual advantages or disadvantages. The average man is inherently stronger than the average woman, but he is no more skillful. Some of the innate differences in adeptness among people can be overcome by hard work: Those who practice more make greater gains.

Most people can practice sports requiring skill and coordination throughout life. Even after aging muscles have lost their elasticity, the brain will remember how to direct the muscles to move. You'll lose some flexibility, speed, strength, and endurance as you grow older, but you'll maintain much of your skill.

GOAL: CLEARER THINKING

Exercising at any time of day can make you more alert. For four to six hours after you finish exercising, your metabolism is increased and you will be better able to concentrate. Many people experience a "low" period at some time of the day, when they feel particularly sluggish and sleepy. For some, this "low time" occurs in late afternoon, when the cortisol concentration in your bloodstream is at its lowest level. (Cortisol, a hormone made by your adrenal glands, promotes alertness. Too much cortisol, on the other hand, can make you either euphoric or depressed.) Others seem to be at ebb tide in the morning, and they become increasingly alert and productive as the day and night progress, reaching a high point around midnight. If you are a "non-morning person," you may be able to improve your morning alertness by exercising first thing in the morning. Of course, if you can't get up in the first place, the prospect of jumping out of bed and running a few miles on a cold winter morning may be too unpleasant to consider. On the other hand, you may find that you feel so invigorated by the experience that it's actually worth sacrificing a bit of sleep.

Exercise causes your body to make several chemicals that promote alertness. Such chemicals include the *catecholamines*—epinephrine (adrenaline) and norepinephrine (noradrenaline). These hormones prepare you for the *fight or flight reaction,* in which your body's increased tension and alertness prepare you for action.

You must become very familiar with your own body. Once you've learned when you hit your mental peaks and valleys, you can plan a regular exercise program to eliminate the valleys and, possibly, raise the peaks even higher.

Many overweight people are sluggish merely from carrying excess baggage. By losing their unnecessary fat, they can improve their alertness. Exercise is, of course, the best way to lose fat. So exercise can promote alertness in several ways.

GOAL: HAPPIER MOODS

Exercise will make you feel good. A great part of this effect is the result of knowing that you look more attractive and have a healthier body. However, other factors contribute to this mood elevation also. Exercise causes your brain and other parts of your body to produce several chemicals that promote feelings of pleasure and well-being. Some of these prevent and relieve pain too. Psychiatrists sometimes prescribe exercise to treat depression. This therapy is probably effective for the same reasons.

Your brain makes many chemicals that affect mood and alertness. The catecholamines have already been mentioned. Other mood-altering hormones include the *endorphins,* which are natural opiates in the sense that they prevent and relieve pain. These chemicals and another one, called *serotonin,* promote a sense of satisfaction and pleasure. Exercise raises your brain's levels of these hormones, making you feel better.

Despite these mood-elevating effects, much remains unknown about why exercise makes us feel good. The major reason for the improved outlook experienced by most regular exercisers is the general sense of well-being that emanates from knowing that you look and feel better and that you have set and achieved new goals.

FINAL THOUGHTS

We've discussed 11 good reasons why everyone should exercise. Of course, only you can select your own goals and priorities. No one has the right to tell you that you need more endurance or speed. If you don't want to engage in competitive sports, there is no reason why you have to, and you owe no one any explanations. Never be embarrassed to engage in any activity that pleases and rewards you, even if you think that others perform that action with greater skill or beauty.

Many people grew up with the mistaken notion that exercise is necessarily unpleasant, and this erroneous concept should be put to rest. The term "exercise" includes many different activities, and we believe that everyone should find the best ones for her own particular goals and rewards.

If you've decided that your exercise goals include more than just the health benefits, you deserve all the encouragement and guidance in the world to achieve your full potential as a competitive athlete.

2 NUTRITION

Ann Grandjean, a nutrition consultant to the United States Olympic Committee, surveyed some top athletes to see how much they knew about nutrition. She found that most of the athletes had misconceptions that could harm their performances. Many thought incorrectly that the following improve performance:

- A high-protein diet
- Large doses of vitamins
- Salt tablets
- Drinking no water during competition.

Even if you are not a serious competitor, you still should understand the basic scientific rules of eating for exercise. This information may save your health. It could even save your life.

A very *high-protein diet* can damage your kidneys and your liver. Your body has no way to store extra protein, so the extra protein that you eat must be degraded by your liver into organic acids and ammonia. These go to your kidneys and pass out in your urine. Large amounts of these protein breakdown products can increase the pressure in your kidney tubules (the delicate filtering structures in your kidneys) and can damage them.

Massive doses of vitamins are poisons. All vitamins have specific functions in your body. When you take in overdoses, these functions are exaggerated. For example, vitamin D is supposed to help your body take in and use calcium. When you overdose on vitamin D, your body can take in too much calcium and you can develop kidney stones and calcium deposits in your muscles. Niacin is supposed to help your liver process sugar. Overdoses of niacin may damage your liver and interfere with your body's ability to process sugar, so that you may develop a diabetic-like condition.

Taking *excessive amounts of salt* (as salt tablets) can thicken your blood and make it more likely to clot. A clot in the blood vessels leading to your heart can cause a heart attack, and a clot in the blood vessels leading to your brain can cause a stroke.

Drinking no water during long-term exercise, particularly on a hot day, can dehydrate you, raise your body temperature uncontrollably, and kill you.

WHAT IS FOOD?

Everything that you eat is made up of the same basic building blocks that make up your body. A sugar that is found in fruits and candies, glucose, is exactly the same as the glucose that circulates in your bloodstream. A protein building block that is found in steak, lysine, is the same as the lysine that is found in your muscles.

Your body cannot absorb the food that you eat until the food has been broken down into its basic building structures. Food is first broken down into its basic components: carbohydrates, proteins, fats, vitamins, minerals, and water. Then, carbohydrates are broken down into their basic units, sugars; proteins are broken down into their basic units, amino acids; and fats are broken down into their basic units, monoglycerides, glycerol, and fatty acids.

Carbohydrates

Carbohydrates are single sugars and sugars in combinations. Fruit contains two single sugars called *glucose* and *fructose.* Table sugar contains the double sugar *sucrose,* which is made of these two sugars (glucose and fructose) bound together. Milk contains the double sugar *lactose,* which is made of two single sugars bound together, glucose and *galactose.* Starch contains thousands or millions of sugars bound together. Fiber contains millions of sugars bound together so tightly that your body is unable to separate them. As a result, fiber is not absorbed into your bloodstream and passes out as waste.

All carbohydrates must first be broken down into single sugars before they can get into your bloodstream. Of all the sugars in nature, only four are absorbed into your bloodstream: glucose, fructose, galactose, and mannose. Only glucose remains in your circulation, though, for the other three are immediately removed from your bloodstream by your liver. These sugars must be converted into glucose before they can reenter your bloodstream. So, all carbohydrates end up as the single sugar glucose, regardless of whether they are from candy, pasta, bread, corn, fruit, or vegetables.

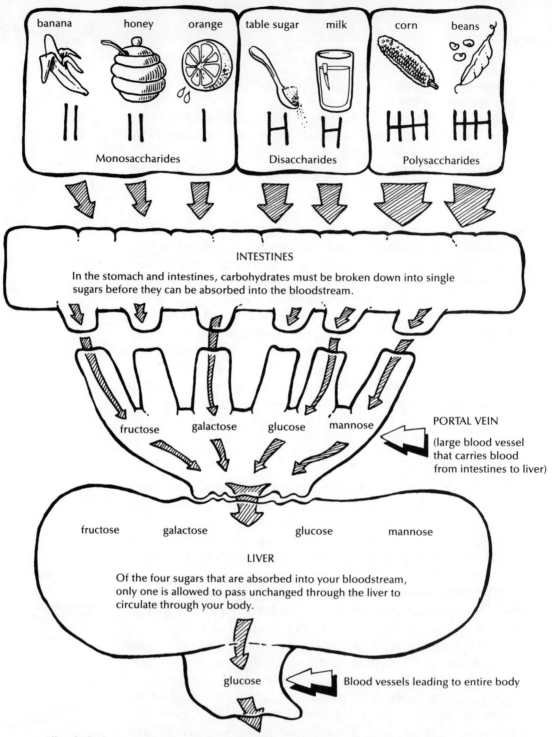

Figure 2-1. How Your Body Processes Carbohydrates. From G. Mirkin, M.D., *Getting Thin*. Boston: Little, Brown & Co., 1983.

Proteins

Proteins are the basic structural materials for all plants and animals. Proteins are made up of basic building blocks called amino acids, which contain the mineral nitrogen. Carbohydrates and fats contain no nitrogen. All of the proteins in nature are made up of 22 amino acids.

Fats

Fats are greasy to touch and are insoluble in water. They are composed of monoglycerides, glycerol, and fatty acids. Eating large amounts of fatty foods may increase your chances of developing cancers of the colon, breast, uterus, bone, and lung. It is also associated with an increased risk of developing a heart attack or stroke.

Vitamins

Most vitamins are parts of chemicals, called enzymes, that help reactions to proceed. For example, chemical A is converted to chemical B, releasing energy in the process. The reaction takes place only if enzyme Q (made up in part by a vitamin) is present. Vitamins help process other nutrients, but they are never a source of energy. It makes no sense to skip a meal and take a vitamin pill in its place. Vitamins must act on other foodstuffs to have any effect on your body.

Minerals

Minerals are basic elements that are found in the soil. They are picked up from the soil by plants. When a woman eats the plants or meat from animals that have eaten the plants, she incorporates the minerals into her own tissues.

Each mineral has specific functions. Calcium makes bones and teeth hard; sodium (salt) regulates the distribution of water in the body; potassium helps to protect your muscles from overheating during exercise; and magnesium helps to regulate the conversion of carbohydrates to energy.

Some minerals are necessary to form the hormones and enzymes that regulate body processes: iodine in thyroid hormone, iron in hemoglobin, zinc in insulin, cobalt in vitamin B_{12}, and sulfur in thiamine and biotin.

The body needs 7 minerals in large amounts and 14 in trace amounts. The following minerals are required in large amounts:

Sodium	Phosphorus
Potassium	Chlorine
Magnesium	Sulfur
Calcium	

The following minerals are required in trace amounts:

Chromium	Molybdenum
Cobalt	Nickel
Copper	Selenium
Fluorine	Silicon
Iodine	Tin
Iron	Vanadium
Manganese	Zinc

Water

Water comprises about half of your body weight. Every cell and organ in your body needs water. Most of your blood volume is composed of water too; it is necessary to keep your blood pressure high enough and to keep your blood circulating to all of your organs properly. The foods you eat contain some water, but you have to drink fluids in order to supply your body with enough water. Because you lose water when you perspire, you need even more water when you are exercising than when you are resting.

HOW YOUR MUSCLES USE FOOD FOR ENERGY

At rest, your muscles burn mostly fat. During exercise, your muscles burn fat and sugar. The harder you exercise, the greater the percentage of sugar that your muscles burn. When you run a 100-yard dash as fast as you can, your muscles use sugar almost exclusively. Protein is not a major source of energy during exercise, so your requirements for protein do not increase significantly when you exercise.

"Hitting the Wall" (Low Muscle Sugar)

How long you can exercise a muscle depends on how much sugar you can store in your muscle and how long you can keep the sugar in your muscle. Stored sugar is called *glycogen*. When a muscle runs out of its stored sugar supply, you will "hit the wall." Your muscle will start to hurt, you will have difficulty coordinating it, and you will feel tired.

Depletion (Training Your Muscles to Store More Sugar)

You can teach your muscles to store more sugar by exercising them until the glycogen is nearly used up. You can tell when this is happening to you because you will feel like you have "hit the wall." Following a depletion workout, your muscles will be able to take up increased amounts of sugar from carbohydrate-containing foods that you eat.

Depletion should not be done more often than once a week. Depleting more often than that can interfere with a normal training program requiring intense exercise at least twice a week. (See Chapter 1.)

The time required for depletion in any sport depends on the fitness of the athlete and the rate at which energy is used in the sport. Top marathon runners can usually run for 2 hours before depleting their muscles of glycogen. The best cyclists take 4 to 6 hours to deplete, and the most skilled cross-country skiers take 12 hours to deplete.

Carbohydrate Packing (Eating So Your Muscles Store More Sugar)

An athlete can increase her endurance by exercising until she has depleted the muscle sugar that she will use in her event and then eating her regular meals plus extra carbohydrates for the next three days. However, recent research has shown that a well-conditioned athlete does not need to manipulate her diet. All she has to do to fill her muscles maximally with glycogen is reduce her training load for 4 days. A marathon runner who is running 20 miles a day can fill her muscles by merely cutting back to 5 miles a day.

Bonking (Low Blood Sugar)

When you are at rest, there is enough sugar in your bloodstream to last for only three minutes. During exercise, your muscles and brain draw sugar rapidly from your bloodstream, depleting your bloodstream of sugar even faster (within a minute). To keep your blood sugar level from falling too low, your liver must constantly release sugar from its cells into your bloodstream. If your liver has not stored enough sugar to continue supplying your bloodstream during exercise, your blood sugar level may drop. If it drops a little, you may become weak and tired. If it drops to very low levels, you may pass out! More than 98% of the energy used to fuel your brain comes from the sugar in your blood. When your blood sugar level falls, your brain cannot function properly. Bicycle racers who do not eat during long races are particularly susceptible to this condition, which is called *bonking.* Other symptoms of bonking include headache, sweating, dizziness, shaking, confusion, and the inability to use your muscles.

The "Last Supper" (Eating on the Night Before)

On the night before a marathon, runners wash their bras (if they wear them), check their running shoes, say their mantras, and eat pasta. They eat pasta to fill their muscles with glycogen.

You cannot depend on the pregame meal to fill your muscles with glycogen. It takes at least 10 hours from the time you eat for your muscles to fill with sugar. Eat your regular meal and make sure that it includes extra carbohydrates. It doesn't make any difference whether you eat candy, pastry, pasta, bread, fruit, or pancakes.

Eating Before Competing (The Pregame Meal)

You *should* eat breakfast three to five hours before a competitive event. As already mentioned, your brain gets more than 98% of its energy from the sugar in your bloodstream. However, there is enough sugar in your bloodstream to last only three minutes. So, your liver must continuously release sugar from its cells into your bloodstream. There is enough sugar in your liver to last only 12 hours at rest, the time that will usually elapse between your "last supper" and "race morning." During exercise, liver sugar is used up at a much more rapid rate.

If you do not eat breakfast, your liver can run out of its stored sugar, reducing your blood sugar level. A low blood sugar level can make you feel tired during exercise, even though you have plenty of calories stored in your body as fat.

Theoretically, your pregame meal shouldn't include fat because fat delays stomach emptying, or protein because its breakdown products are organic acids and urea, both of which are diuretics. You don't want to have a full bladder during competition. However, anything can be included in your pregame meal as long as it has passed out of your stomach by the time you start your competition and does not contain a lot of sugar.

Sugar Before Competing

Do not eat foods that contain a lot of sugar in your pregame meal. You should not have more than one glass of orange juice and you should avoid candy bars, maple syrup, and honey. Recent studies have shown that several potatoes in your pregame meal can also harm your performance. Your body processes the starch in potatoes in the same way it processes sugar.

When you eat a sugar-rich meal, your blood sugar level rises. When it rises high enough, your pancreas produces a hormone called insulin which causes your blood sugar level to drop. The presence of the insulin together with the exertion of your muscles will draw sugar so rapidly from your bloodstream that you can develop a low blood sugar level and become tired.

Your pancreas releases insulin every time your blood sugar level rises high enough. This can happen after you eat anything, and that includes foods containing carbohydrates, fat, or protein. Usually, the insulin that follows a meal will be degraded by your body, primarily in your liver and kidneys, in less than 3 hours. So, you should not take in any food within 3 hours of the start of your competition, but you can safely eat more than 3 hours before the start.

Sugar During Competition

If you are participating in an event that takes less than 3½ hours, you do not need to eat during your competition. Vigorous exercise that takes more than 3½ hours (such as a marathon for some) can use up enough calories to deplete your body sugar stores and make you feel tired. In such events, eating during competition will help you exercise longer.

It is perfectly all right for you to eat sugary foods during exercise. During exercise, the muscles draw sugar from your bloodstream so rapidly that your blood sugar level never gets high enough to cause your pancreas to release insulin.

During long bicycle rides, racers may eat as often as every 15 minutes. Favorite foods in their backpacks include such items as bananas, peanut butter and jelly sandwiches, and chicken.

Eating After Competing

After hard exercise, the stored sugar supply in your muscles will be low, and you will feel tired. Refilling your muscles with glycogen will help you recover from exercise. The average marathon runner takes in about 250 grams of carbohydrates a day, which is not enough to replenish the glycogen lost by your muscles. You need at least 600 grams of carbohydrates each day to replenish muscle glycogen rapidly. So, eating extra carbohydrates after exhaustive exercise will help you recover faster.

Fluids During Exercise

You can improve your performance in any exercise that takes more than 45 minutes by taking fluids when you exercise. This is especially true in hot weather. Jim Counsilman, the famous Indiana University swimming coach, has shown that top swimmers can lose more than 3 pounds (about 3 pints) of fluid through sweating in each hour of swimming.

On warm days, take a cup of cold water a few minutes before you exercise and every 15 minutes during exercise. This will help to prevent dehydration during exercise. The best drink for short-term exercise is cold water, which is less likely to cause cramps than warm water. Cold water causes your stomach to contract, pushing the water into your intestines, where it is absorbed into your bloodstream. Thus, cold water is absorbed more rapidly than warm water.

Minerals During Exercise

You won't need minerals during exercise that takes less than 4 hours. During exercise, your blood potassium level rises slightly because potassium is released from your muscles into your bloodstream. Your blood sodium (salt) level also rises during exercise because sweat contains more water than salt in comparison to your blood. So you lose more water than salt from your bloodstream, causing the salt concentration in your blood to rise. Your blood calcium level remains the same. Because magnesium moves from your bloodstream into your red blood cells when you exercise, your blood magnesium level falls slightly. So you don't need to replace any minerals for short exercise sessions. However, exertion lasting more than 4 hours will lead to some mineral loss. The food you eat to restore your energy will supply you with more than enough minerals to replace your losses.

Sport Drinks, Soft Drinks, and Juices

A sugar concentration of greater than 2.5 percent in an exercise drink will delay the absorption of that drink into your bloodstream. Most sport drinks, juices, and soft drinks have around 10 percent sugar because that is the concentration of sugar in drinks that tastes best. Extra sugar slows absorption, thus keeping your stomach full longer and possibly harming your performance. Since you probably pour some of your drink on your head to help cool you, sweetened drinks offer the additional disadvantage of making your head and shoulders sticky. Thus, cold water remains the best drink during competition. If you don't like the flavorless taste of water or the metallic odor or taste emanating from the minerals present in that water, tea is a refreshing drink to replace your fluid loss.

Drink Before You Are Thirsty

Don't ever wait to drink until you are thirsty. You won't become thirsty until you have already lost 2 to 4 pounds of water and, by then, it's too late to make up the deficit. There are special cells in your brain called osmoreceptors, which tell you when you are thirsty. These cells are called into action only when the concentration of the salt in your bloodstream rises to high levels. Since sweat contains some salt (in addition to water), the concentration of salt in your bloodstream rises more slowly than it would if sweat contained only water. Thus, sweating leads to considerable fluid loss, even though it promotes the thirst signal slowly. By the time you have lost 3 percent of your body weight as fluid, your temperature will have risen and your performance will have deteriorated markedly.

DO YOU NEED MORE PROTEIN FOR EXERCISE?

Protein is not a major source of energy for your muscles. Your muscles burn mostly fat and carbohydrates. They use very little protein. It takes almost as much protein to sit in a chair as it does to run a marathon.

Eating extra protein will not help your muscles grow larger or stronger. The only stimulus to strengthen a muscle is to exercise that muscle against resistance. This stimulus is so great that you can enlarge a muscle while you are fasting, while you are losing weight, and while all of your other muscles are growing smaller.

Eating extra protein can harm you. Your body has no way to store extra protein. So, when you take in more protein than your body can use immediately, your liver breaks down the protein into organic acids and ammonia, both of which are eliminated in your urine. This leads to greater urine production, which can dehydrate you, setting you up for a poor performance, particularly in hot weather. It also can increase your chances of developing heatstroke, a sudden uncontrolled rise in body temperature that can cause you to pass out.

You don't need much extra protein even to enlarge your muscles. For example, 1 pound of muscle contains only about 100 grams of protein, since it is composed of more than 72 percent water. So if you are gaining 1 pound of muscle every week in an excellent strength training program, you are adding only about 100 grams of protein each week, or about 15 grams of protein each day. Two cups of corn and beans will meet this added need—far less than you'd expect.

DO YOU NEED MORE VITAMINS FOR EXERCISE?

Enzymes are not direct participants in chemical reactions, and they usually are present in much greater quantities than needed. So enzymes are rarely used up during the normal chemical reactions of everyday life. Your requirements for them are miniscule. Vitamins last a while in your body, and those that are depleted are easy to replace. Taking more vitamins than are necessary will not make body reactions take place any better or faster. Indeed, the extra vitamins are wasted. For example, more than 80 percent of a 1-gram dose of vitamin C is excreted in your urine shortly after you take it into your body.

Your requirements for only four vitamins increase with exercise: thiamine, niacin, riboflavin, and pantothenic acid. These vitamins are used up minimally in the breakdown of carbohydrates and, to a small degree, protein for energy. But you will find them abundantly in your food. You will even find them in white bread that has had the vitamins removed in the polishing process. According to The Enrichment Act of 1942, white bread and all other grain products that cross state lines must be enriched with the nutrients that were removed during the refining process, including thiamine, niacin, and riboflavin. There is no difference between the vitamins that were there originally and those that were added later. Furthermore, deficiencies of these vitamins have never been reported in athletes.

Can You Overdose on Vitamins?

Too much of any vitamin can be dangerous and even fatal. Vitamins have specific functions in your body. When you take in more than your body needs, these functions can be exaggerated and can harm you. As we mentioned earlier in this chapter, taking large doses of vitamin D can make your body take in too much calcium and can cause you to develop kidney stones and calcium deposits in your muscles. Excessive amounts of niacin can damage your liver and can cause you to develop very high blood sugar levels.

Does Taking Extra Vitamin C Prevent Colds?

There is no evidence that extra vitamin C will protect you from developing a cold. There are at least 13 well-controlled studies which showed that those who take vitamin C have as many colds as those who take no supplements whatever.

DO YOU NEED MORE MINERALS FOR EXERCISE?

With the exception of iron and calcium, female athletes do not need to take mineral supplements.

Iron

Most men get all the iron that they need from the food that they eat. Women would too, if they ate better and did not menstruate. The average menstruating woman needs 18 milligrams of iron a day—6 milligrams to replace the iron that is lost during menstruation and 12 milligrams to replace all the other losses. She takes in only 12 milligrams per day. Inadequate dietary iron and the extra blood lost through menstruation cause one out of every four women in this country to be iron-deficient, although only one in twenty is anemic from lack of iron.

You can be iron-deficient and still not be anemic. Less than 50 percent of the iron in your body is in your red blood cells. The rest is called *iron reserve* and is stored in your bone marrow, liver, spleen, and other tissues.

You will not become anemic from iron deficiency until your body has used up almost all of your iron reserves. Iron deficiency without anemia can prevent you from performing at your best. Iron deficiency, even in the absence of anemia, delays the removal of lactic acid during exercise, and this can cause you to tire earlier. You can find out if you are iron-deficient by having a blood sample drawn for a serum ferritin test.

All female athletes can help to protect themselves from becoming iron-deficient by eating a diet rich in meat, fish, and chicken, all of which have iron in a form that is absorbed easily into your body. The iron in plant foods is not absorbed as well. The average woman can make up for her deficiency by taking three 100-milligram tablets of iron each week.

Calcium

Calcium is necessary for you to have strong bones and teeth. The Recommended Dietary Allowance for calcium is 1,000 milligrams, which you will find in four glasses of milk. However, you do not have to drink milk. You can get calcium from other sources, as listed in the following table:

CALCIUM EQUIVALENTS (250 MG CALCIUM)

1 glass of milk
1 cup of yogurt
1 ounce hard cheese
1 1/2 cups of ice cream
1 1/4 cups of cottage cheese
600-milligram calcium carbonate pill

Regular exercisers who eat a lot of dairy products may get all the calcium they need, but many do not. Many women who do not menstruate (i.e., are *amenorrheic*) lack the female hormone estrogen, which is necessary to help keep calcium in their bones. These women require even more dietary calcium. Some recent studies imply that exercise will not make up for these women's lack of estrogen and will not keep the bones strong by keeping calcium in them. Amenorrheic women may suffer from thin bones that crack easily. (See Chapter 6.)

To help to keep their bones strong, nonmenstruating women should take in foods that contain 1,500 milligrams of calcium rather than just 1,000 milligrams. They should also be checked by a competent gynecologist. Lack of menstruation can be a sign of serious disease such as a tumor and should not be ignored.

Sodium

You can replace the salt you've lost in sweating by merely eating foods which contain salt, even if you're exercising heavily. Regular foods contain so much salt that healthy people tend to consume more salt than they need anyway. Heavy exercisers need about 3,000 milligrams of salt a day. The average American gets between 6,000 and 18,000 milligrams. Manufacturers add salt to food to preserve it. Canned peas contain 300 times as much salt as fresh peas. You add salt to make food taste good. If you were to stop using a saltshaker, stop cooking with salt, and stop eating anything that tastes salty, you would still get about 3,000 milligrams of salt a day.

If you lack salt, you will feel weak and tired, and you may develop muscle cramps, particularly when you exercise in hot weather. Check with your doctor if you have these symptoms. You'll need a blood test to determine if you really lack salt and if you need to take more. Chances are that your blood sodium concentration will be normal.

If you are low on salt, you can usually make up for your deficiency by salting your food. We do not recommend that you take salt tablets. They come in such a concentrated form that they can irritate your stomach and make you feel nauseated. They can also raise the salt concentration in your bloodstream, and this will increase your chances of forming undesirable clots. A clot in the blood vessels leading to your heart can cause a heart attack, a clot in the blood vessels leading to your brain can cause a stroke, and a clot in the blood vessels leading to your kidneys can cause kidney failure.

Potassium

Potassium deficiency almost never occurs in athletes. It is extremely difficult to devise a diet that is too low in potassium, since potassium is found in everything that you eat, including meat, fish, chicken, fruits, vegetables, grains, and nuts. The only food that doesn't have potassium is pure sugar.

Your body requires very little extra potassium for exercise, and a balanced diet provides a healthy person with plenty of potassium. Although potassium deficiency can cause weakness and muscle cramps, it is rarely the cause of these symptoms in healthy people. Taking potassium supplements can raise your blood potassium too high, and this can cause irregular heartbeats.

The most common causes of potassium deficiency are vomiting, diarrhea, laxative abuse, and diuretic use. Several female athletes have come to our offices reporting sudden decreases in athletic performance. They had low blood levels and high urine levels of potassium. All of them had *bulimia,* a condition in which a person eats a full meal and then induces vomiting, as a means of losing weight. (See Chapter 8.) Bulimia can be a sign of a serious underlying emotional problem that requires hospitalization and close medical supervision.

Trace Minerals

There are 14 trace minerals that your body requires in small amounts, in order for you to be healthy. Diseases due to lack of trace minerals are almost unheard of in this country. Plants require nine of the 14 trace minerals that you need. They can't grow without them. Their roots extract minerals from the soil and incorporate them into their fruits, stems, nuts, leaves, and seeds. We get our minerals by eating the plants or the meat of animals who have eaten the plants. So anything that you eat is likely to contain the nine trace minerals that plants require.

There are five trace minerals that plants do not require: iodine, selenium, cobalt, fluorine, and zinc. Plants will pick up these minerals if they are in the soil but will grow without them if they are not in the soil. If you eat foods that are grown only on soil that lacks a specific mineral, your body may lack that mineral. For example, years ago people became deficient in the mineral iodine as a result of eating only plants that were grown on the iodine-deficient soil around the Great Lakes. These people developed goiters (enlarged thyroid glands) and symptoms of underactive thyroid glands. Nowadays, deficiencies of these minerals are rare, even for the five trace minerals that may not be found in plants. Our transportation system is so extensive that we get our oranges from Florida, our pecans from Texas, our potatoes from Idaho, and our cranberries from Washington. It is virtually impossible for all soils to be deficient in the same mineral.

A Mineral-Rich Diet

Scientists have not yet devised a specific pill that contains all the necessary minerals in their proper proportions, not even for the major minerals. Potassium, in pill form, can cause intestinal ulcers; in liquid form it has a foul taste. Unless bound to protein, magnesium cannot be given in pill form because it is poorly absorbed and can cause diarrhea.

Dolomite pills, which contain calcium and magnesium, are used by some athletes. However, some preparations of dolomite contain lead, which is poisonous. Several companies have developed commercial drinks for athletes, but most of them contain less potassium and magnesium than are found in orange juice, and these drinks usually contain no trace elements. At present, the only way you can be sure of getting proper quantities and proportions of all the minerals that you need is by eating a well-balanced diet.

A WELL-BALANCED DIET

Food supplements are not necessary. The easiest system for ensuring adequate nutrition is the Four Food Group Plan developed by the Department of Agriculture in 1956. Although most foods contain a combination of nutrients, this plan groups foods according to their predominant nutritional values. Since the foods in each group are similar to each other in primary food content, you can vary the diet based on these four food groups by choosing different foods within the same group.

The four food groups are as follows:

1. Fruits and vegetables
2. Cereals and grains (including starchy vegetables)
3. High-protein foods (meat, fish, poultry, beans, eggs)
4. Milk and dairy products

The average sedentary woman needs four servings* from each of Groups 1 and 2, and she needs two servings from each of Groups 3 and 4. At least four servings of *each* of the four food groups are needed for the average active exercising woman. Although no two foods ever have precisely the same nutritional value, the foods within each group are similar enough to permit reasonable substitutions while still satisfying all requirements. If you choose widely among the members of each food group and consume at least four servings from each group, you will meet all of your needs and enjoy a balanced, varied diet.

---

*As defined in Hamilton and Whitney, *Nutrition Concepts and Controversies*, West Publishing Co., St. Paul, MN, 1979, page 29, serving sizes are as follows: 1. Fruits and vegetables: 1/2 cup. 2. Cereals and grains: 1 slice bread; 1/2 cup cooked cereal; 1 cup ready-to-eat cereal. 3. High-protein foods: 2-3 ounces of cooked meat, fish, or chicken; 1 cup cooked beans. 4. Milk and dairy products: 1 cup milk; 1-2 ounces cheese.

3 DRUGS

Twenty-three centuries ago, Macedonian competitors drank a potion made up of ground-up hooves of Macedonian asses, boiled in oil and sprinkled with rose petals. Eighty years ago, Tom Hicks won the Olympic marathon and collapsed at the finish line. He didn't come around for some time. He was reported to have used a mixture of strychnine and alcohol to keep him going. You may chuckle when you think of athletes taking ground-up hooves, or strychnine and alcohol. You know that such potions and drugs can't possibly help an athlete. In fact, they can harm both an athlete's performance and her health. Just as useless today are bee pollen, vitamin B_{15} (which may not even exist), spirulina, and a host of other products taken by athletes that have never been shown to boost athletic performance.

ANABOLIC STEROIDS

As we discuss in Chapter 8, boys and girls who participate in the same activities are about equally strong until they reach puberty. Then the boys start to develop larger and stronger muscles. That's the time when the male body starts to produce large amounts of the masculinizing hormone testosterone. The female body produces large amounts of the feminizing hormone estrogen. Because estrogen helps the body to form fat while testosterone causes muscles to become larger and stronger, men have a natural advantage for sports that involve strength.

Anabolic steroids are androgens, which are masculinizing hormones that promote muscle growth. They may be produced naturally in your body or synthetically in a laboratory.

The synthetic hormones are similar to the masculinizing hormones that are naturally produced by both men and women. Men produce much more of these substances than women do, though, so men tend to have larger and stronger muscles than women.

> Twenty years ago I gave out a questionnaire before a race. It asked, "If you could take a pill that would make you an Olympic champion, but may kill you in a year, would you take it?" More than half responded that they would.
>
> —Gabe Mirkin, M.D.

Sex Testing

Until the 1960s, some men competed as women because they realized that this gave them a competitive advantage. Then sex testing was initiated before many international competitions. Such testing is very easy to perform. Some cells are scraped from the inside lining of the cheek, and these cells are tested for *Barr bodies.* The number of Barr bodies in a cell is usually one less than the number of X chromosomes a person has. Thus, normal women, who have two X chromosomes, usually have one Barr body in each cell. Normal men, who have only one X chromosome, usually have no Barr bodies. This test, although easy to perform, is not always accurate and is certainly less accurate than doing a complete chromosome analysis (a *karyotype*), a test which is difficult, time-consuming, and expensive to perform. Besides, a person's chromosomes do not determine the sex in which he or she functions. The best way to determine someone's sex is to see if the person has a penis.

However, the introduction of sex testing by scraping the inside of the cheek changed things dramatically.

The Rise of Anabolic Steroids

Since men were no longer allowed to compete in women's events, athletes and coaches sought ways to make women stronger, as a means of improving a team's competitive edge. It occurred to them that giving women masculinizing hormones might give them an athletic advantage.

The discovery of anabolic steroids is credited to a physician at the University of Alabama, Dr. Charles Kockakian, who first synthesized an anabolic steroid before World War II. He used the drug to prevent protein loss in very old patients. After the war, steroids were given to starved concentration camp survivors to help rebuild their protein

In 1967 the Polish sprinter Ewa Klobukowska flunked her sex test. After that, some of the great "female" athletes stopped competing. What happened to the Roumanian world record holder in the high jump, Iolanda Balas, the Russian sprinter Maria Itkina, and the Olympic champions Irina and Tamara Press?

stores. Because of their proven value in conserving protein in the body in people who do not produce enough of their own testosterone, it was thought that giving healthy people large amounts of anabolic steroids would make them even stronger.

Anabolic steroids *can* make muscles bigger and stronger, provided that they are used along with weight training and provided that the athlete eats enough food to satisfy her calorie and protein needs. However, these findings have not been confirmed with definitive controlled, double-blind studies. (A double-blind study is one in which one group takes the drug, another group takes a placebo, both groups do everything else the same, and neither group knows which is taking the drug and which is taking the placebo.) Subjects taking anabolic steroids can always tell that they are taking these drugs, since they have more drive and energy than they did before. So it is impossible to carry out a double-blind study using anabolic steroids. As a result, the beneficial effects of these drugs have not yet been proven conclusively. Some of the muscle enlargement associated with their use is probably due to water retention, and some of the gains in muscle size and strength are undoubtedly due to increased training as a result of greater drive and energy. So the effects are much more complex than they at first appear.

Among the great athletes who have been caught taking steroids are Natalia Marasescu (Roumanian world record holder in the mile), Ileana Silai (Roumanian 1968 Olympic silver medalist in the 800-meter run), and Totka Petrova (Bulgarian 1979 World Cup 1500-meter champion).

A review of scientific studies shows that people who take anabolic steroids and do not exercise against resistance do not become stronger. Novice athletes also do not become stronger when they take anabolic steroids. However, most world-class weight lifters feel that anabolic steroids help to make them stronger. It is the people who are already working at their maximum that may be helped.

Drug Testing

Although it isn't known whether anabolic steroids actually improve athletic performance, many athletes believe that they do and also believe that they will be at a disadvantage if they do not use the drugs. However, it is illegal and unethical to use anabolic steroids for athletic gain. Urine tests are routinely performed to detect these drugs, and the tests are now so sensitive and reliable that it is nearly impossible to use anabolic steroids without being detected.

What Are the Dangers?

Although the benefits of anabolic steroids haven't been proven conclusively, several dangers have been proven. Most of the studies have been done in men because fewer women are using them and even fewer are admitting that they do. The adverse effects upon the reproductive systems are different for men and women. Although most adverse effects on other parts of the body have been found in studies of men, similar effects are expected to occur in women.

Some of the bad effects are related to liver damage, which occurs occasionally and can be fatal. Your liver processes the steroids present in your body, both those made by your body and those taken as medication. While your liver can handle the amounts normally made by your body, it may not be able to process the massive doses taken by some athletes. Liver damage and even cancer have been reported among healthy athletes taking these drugs.

In addition to the risk of liver damage, anabolic steroids increase your chances of having a heart attack or stroke. As we discuss in Chapter 9, masculinizing hormones have an adverse effect on the ratio of beneficial high-density lipoprotein (HDL) cholesterol to harmful low-density lipoprotein (LDL) cholesterol. They lower the good HDL and raise the bad LDL, increasing your chances of having a heart attack or stroke. Both debilitated older people and young healthy athletes are more likely to have heart attacks while taking anabolic steroids. Since women usually have more good HDL and less bad LDL then men to start with, these adverse effects of anabolic steroids may be less for women than for men. However, a lower cardiovascular risk for women remains speculative and has not yet been shown in scientific studies.

It may take a long time to accumulate enough information to resolve this question. Plaques are laid down in arteries very slowly. It takes years for enough plaque to form to completely block an artery in your heart to cause a heart attack, or to completely block an artery in your head to cause a stroke. We may learn more about these ill effects in the future, after more scientific studies have accumulated information about athletes using anabolic steroids for a longer time.

In men, anabolic steroids can cause a decrease in sperm production and testicular size. Normally, a man's pituitary gland makes hormones that stimulate his testicles. The pituitary gland makes more of its hormones when a man's testosterone level is low and makes less of its hormones when a man's testosterone level is high. The high level of anabolic steroids in his blood tells his pituitary gland to make less of its hormones. When his testicles are no longer stimulated, they shrink and make less testosterone and fewer sperm. (Note that this decrease in sperm production does not make anabolic steroids a reliable method of contraception.) However, as long as a man is taking synthetic masculinizing hormones, his sex drive and potency should be fine or possibly even enhanced!

Women can be masculinized by anabolic steroids. This means that if you take these drugs you can develop excessive facial and body hair, acne, male-pattern baldness, deepening of your voice, and enlargement of your clitoris. Some of these problems are only temporary and should resolve when you stop using the anabolic steroid, but others are permanent. Dark, abundant facial and body hair will not fall out. An enlarged clitoris will not shrink. A deep voice will not get higher in pitch. Acne will probably clear up, and your receding hairline will probably return to normal when you stop using these drugs.

Anabolic steroids adversely affect the menstrual cycle too. They can cause a luteal phase defect (with partial progesterone deficiency) or anovulation (with total progesterone deficiency). If taken in large enough doses or for a long enough time, they can probably cause amenorrhea too (with estrogen and progesterone deficiency). These conditions are discussed in detail in Chapter 6. Most menstrual abnormalities that result from using anabolic steroids are probably temporary. If you had normal ovulation and menstruation before you used these drugs, you will probably be able to have children when you want to, after stopping these agents.

Will Prescribed Hormones be Detected by Screening Tests?

As we discuss in Chapter 10, the drug danazol, which is used to treat endometriosis, is an anabolic steroid. This will be detected in the routine screening tests. So competitive athletes who are taking this drug for medical reasons must choose between competing and treating their disease. If they want to compete, they should switch to medroxyprogesterone acetate or to birth control pills at least three months before competition. Neither of these will be detected in the tests used to screen athletes. Birth control pills, when taken in usual amounts prescribed for contraception or replacement of hormone deficiencies, also will not be detected in the tests used to screen athletes.

GROWTH HORMONE

Growth hormone is now being used by many athletes. It is a protein hormone that is normally made by your pituitary gland. Children who lack this hormone remain small and short as adults. Giving growth hormone to children who lack it can certainly increase their size and strength. However, it isn't known whether giving more growth hormone to people who already have enough will make them larger and stronger too. Growth hormone does increase protein synthesis, and this is the first step toward enlarging and strengthening muscles.

Although the benefits of growth hormone to athletes haven't been proven in controlled studies, some adverse effects are known. For example, it reduces the amount of sugar leaving your bloodstream to enter muscle cells and thus raises your blood sugar level. This may lead to diabetes. It can also cause retention of sodium, chloride, potassium, magnesium, phosphorous, and calcium. These may interfere with your normal body functions. There is a condition, called acromegaly, in which the pituitary gland produces too much growth hormone. Those who have this disease develop very coarse features due to thickening of their bones. Although thickening is desirable if it strengthens bones, people with this disease do not have strong

ADVERSE EFFECTS OF ANABOLIC STEROIDS

Increased risk of liver damage and liver cancer
Increased risk of heart attack or stroke
Acne
Excessive facial and body hair
Enlargement of the clitoris
Deepening of the voice
Male-pattern baldness
Menstrual irregularity and amenorrhea
Infertility
Fluid retention
High blood pressure
(Short stature, when given to children)
(Decreased sperm production and testicular size, when
    given to men)

bones, and they often develop osteoporosis. They often perspire excessively, develop excessive skin pigmentation, and have joint pains.

Scientists do not know if these same adverse effects will occur in those taking growth hormone supplements. The fact that these adverse effects have not been reported in athletes yet may be because athletes tend to use safe amounts of growth hormone, or it may be because growth hormone use among athletes has not been studied long enough. However, until it is known how much of this drug is safe and how much is excessive, we believe that the potential dangers exceed the potential benefits.

At one time, the only source of growth hormone was the pituitary glands of cadavers. As a consequence the supply was very limited and was reserved primarily for children who lacked the hormone. Now it can be manufactured in abundance by bacteria, and it will be much more readily available as a result. Synthetic growth hormone is almost exactly like that which is made by the human body, so drug tests do not distinguish whether the growth hormone in a person's body was produced naturally or was taken by injection. Unlike anabolic steroids, which can remain in a person's body for several weeks or even months, growth hormone is eliminated from the body within minutes.

UPPERS

This category of drugs includes amphetamines, cocaine, caffeine, nicotine, and ginseng. They differ from one another in several respects—their chemical makeup, how they are administered, how fast and how long they work, and how dangerous they are—but they all work in the same way. They stimulate your central nervous system by causing your body to produce more of its own natural stimulant, adrenaline, and by making your body more sensitive to this hormone.

What They Do

Adrenaline—also called *epinephrine*—is made by your body all the time. Its levels in your bloodstream rise naturally when you experience a very strong emotion, such as fear, rage, or excitement. It prepares your body for action. For example, when you fight, you need more blood to be sent to your brain (to think), your lungs (to take in more oxygen), your muscles (to move your body), your heart (to pump more blood), and your skin (to cool your body). Therefore, adrenaline opens up the blood vessels to these parts of your body.

To help you act quickly, the blood supply to the parts of your body that you won't be using shuts down. The blood vessels to the stomach, the intestines, and the kidneys constrict.

Side Effects

Your body isn't designed to respond to crisis all the time. Neither is it prepared to be stimulated frequently by drugs that prepare you for the "fight or flight" reaction. Very high levels of stimulants can cause panic, irrationality, extreme aggressiveness and hostility, hyperactive mental and physical behavior, and even psychosis. Too much adrenaline also can strain your heart. It can affect your mind so that you ignore your body's warning signals of pain and fatigue, which may lead you to injure yourself seriously.

All stimulants tend to become less effective as you keep on taking them. As you respond less to the drug, you need higher doses to get the same effect.

All stimulants are habit-forming or addictive. With addiction, your body develops a need for the drug, and its absence causes you to become sick. With a habit-forming drug, you want to keep on taking it.

No stimulants help your performance in any physical way, although they may help you keep on going by causing you to ignore pain. All stimulants can hurt you. Some of them can kill you.

Amphetamines

On a hot day during the 1967 Tour de France, England's Tom Simpson pedaled himself to death. At that time, he was one of the top bicycle racers in the world. A few years before, a high school boy died in a road race. They had taken amphetamine-like stimulants before they raced.

Amphetamines don't make you stronger, faster, better-coordinated, or able to exercise for longer periods. They just make you *think* you are doing better than you are.

Several thousand years ago Publius Syrus wrote, "It is better to learn caution from the misfortune of others, rather than from your own mistakes."

In 1965 I started to run again after a 10-year layoff. One of my first races was a four-miler in Arlington, Virginia. It was my first race in intense heat. The temperature was more than 90 degrees Fahrenheit and there was no water on the course.

By the three-mile mark, my mouth was parched and my chest and legs felt like they were being prodded by red-hot pokers. I felt as if the air that I was breathing came from a hot furnace. I felt dizzy, my head ached, and I suddenly couldn't see. I crossed the finish line and immediately collapsed, suffering from heatstroke. That was almost my last race. It was almost the end of my life.

I don't need to ask myself why I endured the horrible pain leading up to heatstroke. I, as a physician, should have paid attention to some of the warning signs of impending heatstroke as they progressed. I ignored them because I had taken amphetamines before the race.

—Gabe Mirkin, M.D.

Jim Bouton, in his book *Ball Four*, described a pitcher who refused to be taken out of a game because he thought he was pitching so well. He had thrown three home-run balls.

Cocaine

Like amphetamine, cocaine produces euphoria. It can turn an aggressive field-hockey player into a raving maniac who fears no one. It doesn't make you a better athlete. It only makes you *think* you are doing better than you are.

Cocaine comes from a plant grown in South America, where mountain people have used it for centuries to help them to keep going when they are exhausted.

After snorting cocaine, you're stimulated for 20 to 40 minutes. That means you have to snort repeatedly during a competitive event in order to keep yourself stimulated for the entire event. If you take it by mouth, the stimulation lasts a few hours. However, most of the ingested cocaine is broken down by your liver before it gets into your circulation, so much larger doses of ingested cocaine are needed to give you the same high. After you inject it, you're stimulated for 10 to 15 minutes, but the high that it produces is explosive. We can't conceive of athletes shooting cocaine before competition.

Caffeine

Caffeine is a chemical that is found in certain plants. It is contained in food and drink made from these plants or their derivatives: coffee, tea, chocolate, and many soft drinks, particularly colas.

Studies by Dr. David Costill, Director of the Human Performance Laboratory at Ball State University in Muncie, Indiana, have shown that giving caffeine to bicycle racers helps them to exercise longer in the laboratory. However, it probably won't help them in races.

As we mentioned in Chapter 2, your muscles "hit the wall" when they run out of their stored sugar supply. Your muscles burn both fat and sugar for energy. If your muscles could burn more fat, they would burn less sugar and would take longer to run out of their stored sugar.

Caffeine causes fat to leave fat cells and go into your bloodstream. It also causes your muscles to burn more fat and less sugar. So, you would expect your muscles to keep their stored sugar longer and, as a result, be able to exercise longer.

So, will caffeine help you to exercise longer? No, it won't. Caffeine does not act directly on the muscles to increase endurance. It causes your body to produce more adrenaline and makes your body more sensitive to the adrenaline that is produced. It is the adrenaline, and not the caffeine directly, that causes fat to leave the fat cells and enter the bloodstream. It is the adrenaline that causes your muscles to burn more fat and less sugar.

When you pedal a bicycle in the laboratory, you're usually not excited, so you won't have much adrenaline circulating in your bloodstream. In this unexcited condition in the laboratory, the caffeine will increase your adrenaline levels and can help you to exercise longer.

Things are different before a competition. You already know this. When you stand on the starting line before a race, your heart beats rapidly because adrenaline levels in your bloodstream are extremely high. You may have so much adrenaline that the extra adrenaline prompted by the caffeine will just make you shaky. More is not necessarily better and may, in fact, be worse.

Ginseng

Reports have circulated in several nonscientific journals that the East Germans and Russians develop great athletes because they take ginseng. This is nonsense. Ginseng comes from the root of a specific plant. It contains certain chemicals called dametrene triol glycosides. These chemicals are similar to other stimulants found in nature, such as the nicotine in the tobacco leaf and the caffeine in the plants that are used to make coffee, chocolate, and tea.

Like caffeine and nicotine, the damatrene triol glycosides also make your body produce more adrenaline. In low doses, they can improve your concentration, speed up your heart, and give you a feeling of power. In high doses, they can cause insomnia and shakiness and can make you irritable and argumentative. Many women stop menstruating when they take these drugs. There is no evidence that they will make you a better athlete, although they may help you to *think* that you are.

Tobacco

Smoking Tobacco

There's no debate in the scientific community. Smoking tobacco interferes with exercise. When you smoke, you inhale a gas called carbon monoxide, which is absorbed into your bloodstream and binds to your red blood cells so tightly that these cells cannot carry oxygen. The average one-pack-a-day smoker loses as much as 7 percent of her red blood cells to carbon monoxide binding. That means that the blood of a smoker has a 7 percent reduction in its ability to transport oxygen. Because of this, she will tire earlier during exercise.

Smoking cigarettes leads to a chemical addiction, in which your brain becomes accustomed to a certain level of nicotine. You experience withdrawal symptoms every time the level falls, including tension, irritability, anxiety, depression, difficulty in concentrating, tiredness, craving for another cigarette, a tendency to overeat, insomnia, and sweating. Regular exercise often helps to relieve many of these symptoms, even in nonsmokers, and many smokers have found that exercise helped them quit.

Exercise alone may not be adequate, though. If you're trying to break this addiction, you'll need helpful and supportive friends, as well as many distracting outlets for your tension and anxiety. The first week will be the most difficult, as your brain and nerves adjust to the lack of nicotine stimulation. You may need tranquilizers to help you past this biggest hurdle. By the time two to four weeks have passed, all withdrawal symptoms should be gone, and you can take pride in a very difficult accomplishment.

Chewing Tobacco

Some baseball players chew tobacco. Many of them do it to make themselves more alert. Tobacco contains nicotine, which is a potent stimulant, and chewers can absorb far more nicotine than smokers without getting sick.

All of the nicotine in the smoke that you draw into your lungs is absorbed into your bloodstream. The nicotine-rich blood from your lungs travels undiluted right to your brain. Within eight seconds after you puff on a cigarette, almost 100 percent of the inhaled nicotine is inside your brain. You have to limit the amount of nicotine that you take in. If you take your next puff too soon, the next bolus of nicotine will get into your brain before the previous one is used up. Then you will feel dizzy or nauseated.

On the other hand, you can keep chewing all day without getting sick. The nicotine in chewing tobacco is absorbed slowly and continuously through your cheeks and gums. The blood from that area must go back to your heart where it is diluted by blood from the rest of your body before it can get into your brain.

Although the nicotine absorbed by baseball players improves their alertness, there is no evidence that it improves their performance.

MOOD DRUGS

Mood drugs can change your state of mind. They can alter your perception so that things may not always be what they seem to be. The most commonly used mood drugs are alcohol and marijuana.

Alcohol

There is no way that alcohol can help you to become a better athlete. Alcohol decreases the force of your heart's contraction. It increases the amount of oxygen that your heart needs. It decreases the flow of blood to your muscles. It causes your muscles to burn more sugar and less fat, so that they run out of their stored sugar supply earlier. It makes you sweat more so that you are more likely to become dehydrated.

Every once in a while a story appears in a running magazine about a runner who tires during a race, drinks alcohol, and then is rejuvenated so that she passes hundreds of other runners as she flies toward the finish line. Alcohol affects your mind. It's more likely that she only *thought* that she was passing other runners, when, in fact, they were passing her.

Frank Shorter was rumored to have drunk a large amount of beer the night before winning the 1972 Olympic marathon. Alcohol affects athletic performance only when it is in the brain and muscles. It does not impair performance after it has left the bloodstream. The liver breaks down alcohol at a constant rate. In one hour it removes:

- 2/3 jigger of alcohol
- 5 ounces of wine
- 12 ounces of beer

I don't care what the evidence is. Alcohol helped *me* during a race.

Twenty years ago when marathons were less crowded, people of the same ability would run race after race competing specifically against each other. My goal was to beat a runner who usually finished about 10 minutes ahead of me. I had never beaten him.

Right from the start I did everything I could to keep up with him. When he surged, I surged. When he slowed down, I slowed down. At 18 miles, I couldn't keep up and he pulled away from me.

When he was more than a quarter of a mile ahead of me, someone handed him two cans of beer. While he was drinking the second can, I passed him and didn't see him again until long after I had crossed the finish line.

—Gabe Mirkin, M.D.

For alcohol to have been in Frank Shorter's bloodstream at race time, he would have had to have drunk more than twelve 12-ounce cans of beer. He hadn't.

Marijuana

There are lots of things that you can do to make yourself a better runner, but running "on grass" is not one of them. Pot smoking can tire you more quickly *while* you exercise and can increase the time it takes for you to recover *after* you exercise.

Marijuana can make you feel good. It helps you to relax, but it can also damage your lungs and interfere with the process by which your lungs take in and carry oxygen during exercise. One joint will cause as much damage as 16 cigarettes. Tetrahydrocannabinol (THC), the active ingredient in marijuana, attaches to the inhaled carbon particles far more tightly than nicotine does. The marijuana smoker has to work much harder than the cigarette smoker to bring the active ingredient into her lungs. Marijuana smokers suck harder, take deeper breaths and hold the smoke in their lungs for longer periods of time.

If you try to exercise after smoking marijuana, your heart will beat faster than normal while you exercise and it will take longer for your heart rate to return to normal after you finish exercising. The increase in heart rate is related to the dose. Edward Avakian at the University of California in Santa Barbara showed that smoking one joint of marijuana increased heart rate 34% at rest, 18% during exercise, and 50% during recovery.

Even though your heart beats faster when you exercise after smoking marijuana, it does not pump with more force and it does not circulate more blood.

When you exercise, your muscles press against the veins near them and squeeze the blood from the veins back towards your heart. This causes more blood to return to your heart, which makes your heart beat faster and with more force. So, your heart pumps more blood with each contraction and beats more frequently. Marijuana speeds up the heart by stimulating the nerves that speed up the heart rate. It does not cause more blood to return to the heart, so it does not make the heart beat with more force. What you gain by a faster heart rate, you lose because your heart does not pump as much blood with each contraction. So, after smoking marijuana, your heart works harder to pump the same amount of blood, and you will tire earlier.

Marijuana can also damage cell membranes, so the muscle soreness that you feel after you exercise will last longer, and it will take you longer to recover.

Marijuana may make you feel better before you start to exercise, but you will feel worse after you finish.

COLD PILLS

Most over-the-counter cold pills contain an antihistamine and a decongestant. These ingredients help to shrink some of the swelling in your nose and decrease some of the secretions. Cold pills may help to make you feel more comfortable during rest, but they don't help much during exercise.

During exercise, you breathe mostly through your mouth, not your nose. The opening in the back of your throat contains 10 times as much cross-sectional area as the two openings in your nose. Your nostrils are too small to take in enough air during exercise. The opening in the back of your throat is so large that it will permit all the air that you need to pass. Since stuffiness in your nose is not a problem during exercise, a decongestant is unnecessary. The antihistamine in these pills can tire you and make exercise more difficult. For this reason cold pills harm your performance.

DIURETICS

Diuretics are drugs that act on your kidneys to make you excrete salt and water. Exercisers who take them can become deficient in salt (sodium) or potassium, and they can become dehydrated too.

Many people take diuretics to treat high blood pressure or other problems involving fluid retention. Excess fluids can raise your blood pressure by increasing your blood volume. Diuretics decrease the amount of fluid in your bloodstream, thereby lowering blood pressure.

During exercise, you lose fluid at an alarming rate. Swimmers can lose as much as three pints of fluid as sweat during a hard one-hour workout. Low fluid levels tire you and increase your chances of passing out from heatstroke. (See Chapter 4.)

Most diuretics act on your kidneys to force potassium into your urine (and out of your body). If you develop a low body level of potassium, you will be very tired and your muscles will hurt and cramp. Worse than that, your heart can start to beat irregularly.

Regular exercisers should try to avoid diuretics. If your doctor feels that you should take them, make sure that you drink plenty of fluids and check with a doctor immediately if you feel excessively tired, since you may have a low potassium level. You should always drink extra fluids when you take diuretics. Most diuretics remove extra salt from your body, so your body will not retain extra fluid.

ANTIBIOTICS

Antibiotics help your body to fight infections. Scientists have not tested how most antibiotics affect strength, speed, endurance, or coordination. Ampicillin, penicillin, and tetracycline have been tested and have been found to cause no adverse effects.

DMSO

Some extravagant claims have been made about dimethyl sulfoxide (DMSO). Though it is an excellent pain reliever, it has not been shown to help your body to heal faster.

Dimethyl sulfoxide can stop pain without making you feel numb. It acts on the nerves that transmit pain, without blocking feeling. It also does not have to be injected. When DMSO is placed on the skin, it goes through the skin and into the fat underneath. Then it passes into the blood vessels in the fat and circulates through the bloodstream to your muscles. It does not pass from the skin directly into the muscles underneath. You can apply DMSO on the skin on one arm to treat the other arm.

Although DMSO itself does not appear to be a dangerous drug, you must be very cautious about your source. Dimethyl sulfoxide is found in a natural by-product from the paper industry and is available at very little cost. This by-product contains large amounts of known cancer-causing chemicals in addition to the DMSO, which can be carried with the DMSO into your bloodstream. You must be sure to get a pure, medical-grade type of DMSO that does not contain any contaminants. The drug itself appears to be safe, although on rare occasions it can break red blood cells and can damage the liver. Eye problems have been reported in animals but have not been demonstrated in humans.

If you decide to use DMSO, make sure that you clean off the area of the skin that will receive the drug. You must apply enough DMSO, in a thick coating, to completely cover at least one-eighth of your body surface. This turns out to be a whole arm or leg. After you have applied enough DMSO to completely cover the skin area you have selected, cover the area with a white gauze pad for at least three hours. Don't let any fabrics with colored dyes touch the area because the DMSO can carry the dye into your bloodstream.

ASPIRIN-LIKE DRUGS

All exercisers feel some muscle soreness on the day after they exercise vigorously. Aspirin can help to prevent and alleviate some of the soreness which follows vigorous exercise. However, it will not block the pain that accompanies an injury. Therefore, if you take aspirin to help relieve muscle soreness and you still feel pain when you exercise, stop exercising. Most likely you have an injury and continued exercise will only injure you further.

Exercising muscles produce certain chemicals, called prostaglandins. It is believed that these chemicals cause muscle soreness. Aspirin blocks the production of prostaglandins and can help to prevent and treat some of the soreness. However, aspirin will not block the pain caused by muscle injuries. Each muscle is made up of thousands of small stringy fibers. A muscle is injured when some or all of the fibers are torn. The pain of an injury is due to damage to nerve fibers which are torn along with the muscle fibers.

Some women take aspirin prior to exercising to help to prevent some of the soreness that they feel during and after they exercise. They should be aware of the following side effects: aspirin dehydrates you by two mechanisms. It makes you sweat and urinate more. Normally, you lower your body temperature by decreasing your production of heat or accelerating your loss of heat. Aspirin lowers your body temperature by making you sweat more, thereby accelerating your loss of heat. It does not slow down your metabolism. It can also make you sweat more when you exercise, making you more susceptible to dehydration. Aspirin also increases urination by limiting reabsorption of water by the tiny tubules in your kidneys.

Taking one or two aspirin tablets before you exercise isn't likely to hurt you unless you're going to exercise intensely for more than an hour without drinking extra fluids. If you decide to take aspirin before you exercise, make sure that you pay extra attention to drinking fluids while you exercise.

Other possible side effects of aspirin are listed below.

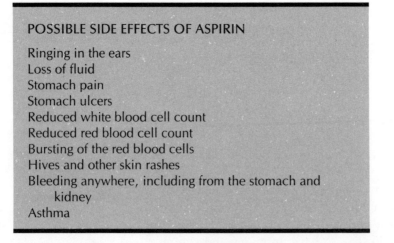

POSSIBLE SIDE EFFECTS OF ASPIRIN

Ringing in the ears
Loss of fluid
Stomach pain
Stomach ulcers
Reduced white blood cell count
Reduced red blood cell count
Bursting of the red blood cells
Hives and other skin rashes
Bleeding anywhere, including from the stomach and
	kidney
Asthma

There are many drugs that act in the same way as aspirin, but are much more effective. These drugs are called *nonsteroidal anti-inflammatory drugs*. They can have the same side effects as aspirin. These drugs include:

Ponstel	Indocin
Nalfon	Tandearil
Motrin	Oxalid
Naprosyn	Clinoral
Zomax	Tolectin
Butazolidine	

(Some of these drugs are recommended for relief and prevention of menstrual cramps, as discussed in Chapter 6.)

BETA BLOCKERS

When you exercise, your body undergoes a number of changes. Large amounts of blood must be pumped to the tissues that will do the most work during exercise and less blood should be pumped to the tissues that aren't used as much. A widening occurs in the blood vessels leading to skeletal muscles, heart, and lungs. The blood vessels leading to your intestines, bladder, and kidney close down. The tubes that carry air to and from your lungs widen so that you can get more oxygen. Your pupils (the darker spots in the middle of your eyes) widen so that you can see better.

All of these reactions are caused by an involuntary nervous system, called the sympathetic nervous system. This system is further subdivided into sympathetic type alpha responders and sympathetic type beta responders. The alpha system constricts the blood vessels in skeletal muscles and widens those in the intestines. The beta system relaxes the blood vessels in involuntary muscles and stimulates the heart.

Noradrenaline is an example of one of the body's natural stimulants that act primarily on the alpha responders, while adrenaline acts more forcibly on the beta responders.

EXAMPLES OF BETA BLOCKERS

Brand Name	*Generic Name*
Blocadron	Timolol
Corguard	Nadolol
Inderal	Propranolol
Lopressor	Metoprolol
Tenormin	Atenolol

When you exercise, your body produces large amounts of adrenaline and noradrenaline. They can make your hands shake, your heart race, and your blood pressure rise. The beta blockers prevent your body from responding to some of the beta effects of adrenaline.

People with irregular heart beats are given beta blockers to stabilize the nerves in the heart so that the heart is less likely to beat irregularly. They are given to people who have angina, which is heart pain caused by lack of oxygen, to reduce the amount of oxygen that the heart requires. They are also given to people who have high blood pressure, to lower the blood pressure by making the heart beat with less force. Beta blockers are also prescribed to prevent migraine headaches, by constricting the blood vessels leading to the brain.

Beta blockers are used by pistol shooters and archers to steady their hands, and by sky divers and sky jumpers to calm them down. Some people take these drugs to prevent anxiety in situations that usually promote anxiety, such as speaking to a large, important audience or taking an important exam.

Beta blockers slow the heart rate during exercise. As discussed in Chapter 1, to become fit you need to exercise vigorously enough to raise your heart rate to more than 120 beats a minute. People on beta blockers can train their hearts at rates much lower than that.

Beta blockers won't inhibit strength, speed or coordination, but they can limit endurance. Although they will not prevent you from exercising, you will tire earlier when you do exercise. For that reason, regular exercisers should try to use other drugs instead of beta blockers for treating any of the problems listed above.

4 THE WEATHER

You can decide when you want to exercise, but you can't control the weather. Obviously, you have to take special precautions when you exercise in very hot or very cold weather. Exercise in very hot weather can cause cramps, loss of fluid, loss of consciousness, and even death. Exercise in very cold weather can cause frostbite and a drop in body temperature that can kill you.

However, these problems should never happen to you. There are many things you can do to avoid weather-related problems, and there is a definite sequence of warning signals that tell you when you are getting into trouble.

When you finish reading this chapter, you will have sufficient knowledge to protect yourself from weather-related injury.

HOT WEATHER

During exercise more than 70 percent of the energy that is used to power your muscles is lost as heat. Less than 30 percent actually powers your muscles. The harder you exercise, the more heat your body produces. Normally, heat is carried from your hot muscles by blood that is pumped to your skin. You perspire and the sweat evaporates from your skin to cool your body. When the weather is hot and the humidity is high, evaporation is not as efficient in keeping you cool, and your body can overheat.

ACCLIMATIZATION

Be very careful during the first few days that you exercise in the heat. It takes at least seven days for your body to adjust to hot-weather exercise. As you acclimatize to the heat, your sweat glands enlarge and you sweat sooner during exercise. Your sweat also becomes saltier. The blood vessels in your skin enlarge so that more blood can get to the skin's surface.

The best protection against hot-weather illness is physical fitness. When you exercise, your heart must pump large amounts of blood to supply oxygen to your exercising muscles. Your heart must also pump large amounts of hot blood from your exercising muscles to your skin, where the heat can be dissipated. The stronger your heart, the more efficiently it can perform these two functions and the better protected you will be against heatstroke.

You don't have to exercise in hot weather to become acclimatized to the heat. During the 1964 trials to pick three members for the United States Olympic marathon team, the temperature rose above 100 degrees Fahrenheit. Buddy Edelin won that race by more than 20 minutes, the largest winning margin ever in a major race. He did this in spite of the fact that he did all of his training in cold England. He acclimatized to the heat by being in shape and training in five sweat suits. It's sweating itself that protects you against heat-caused illness.

SALT TABLETS

Never take salt tablets unless they are recommended by a physician who treats a lot of athletes. Having too much salt is far more dangerous than not having enough. If you take in much more salt than you need, the concentration of salt in your bloodstream can rise, thickening your blood so that it is more likely to clot. A clot in the arteries leading to your heart can cause a heart attack. A clot in the blood vessels leading to your brain can cause a stroke. Having too much salt can also dehydrate you. It makes your kidneys pass more water, so that less is left in your body.

HEAT CRAMPS

Cramps that occur after you have exercised for a long time in the heat are usually caused by dehydration. Cramps that occur both during exercise and during rest are usually due to low blood levels of salt (sodium). They can also be due to a blocked blood vessel (rare in healthy women), a pinched nerve (pinched between two bones or two large muscles, for instance), or low body levels of calcium or potassium. (See cramps, Chapter 13.)

> **Treatment for a Cramped Muscle**
>
> • When you get a cramp, stretch the cramped muscle with one hand and gently knead it with the fingers of your other hand.
> • To prevent cramps, try drinking a cup of water just before you exercise in hot weather and every 15 minutes during exercise.
> • If a cramp recurs, check with your doctor to see if you have low blood levels of minerals, a pinched nerve, or a blocked blood supply.

During exercise, you may lose so much water that there is not enough blood to flow to your exercising muscles. Then the muscles that are being exercised heavily can suffer from lack of oxygen and can go into a painful spasm.

On rare occasions, you may not be taking in enough salt to replace the salt that you lose. However, the average American diet contains 30 to 90 times as much salt as you need, so it is very rare for salt deficiency to occur in healthy American women. Low body levels of potassium and calcium occur only on very rare occasions. Low body levels of calcium are usually caused by abnormal parathyroid glands or kidneys. Low potassium levels are usually caused by vomiting and diarrhea or taking diuretics or large amounts of licorice.

HEAT EXHAUSTION

Figure 4-1. Treatment for a Cramp of the Calf Muscle.

Heat exhaustion is a condition in which your body has too little water. Sixty-five percent of your body weight is water. During exercise you lose tremendous amounts of water. Champion swimmers lose 3 pounds of water per hour from sweating while they swim. Long-distance runners and champion tennis players can lose as many as 5 pounds of water per hour on a very hot day.

So if you exercise for a long period of time without replacing your lost water, you can lose so much water that your blood volume will be reduced and your heart can't do its main job of pumping blood through your body. Without delivery of hot blood from your muscles

Sally R. came to see me as a patient. She was a 16-year-old high-school soccer player who started to work out twice a day to prepare her body for fall practice. After one week of two-a-day workouts, she suddenly became very tired, lost her appetite, and felt that she was sick. She had a temperature of 101 degrees Fahrenheit, large lymph nodes in her armpits, neck, and groin, and a resting heart rate of 100. I thought that she had mononucleosis. However, her mono test was negative. She had heat exhaustion. She stopped exercising for a week, drank plenty of fluids, stayed in air conditioning for a few days, and recovered completely.

—Mona Shangold, M.D.

to your skin for cooling, your temperature can rise dangerously high. You may not have enough circulating blood to supply your brain adequately, and you may pass out as a result.

You can also develop a water shortage slowly over several days. You lose water during exercise and you may not replace all of it. Then on the next day, you exercise and lose more water.

Can You Depend on Thirst?

You can't always depend on thirst to tell you when you need extra fluid. As we discussed in Chapter 2, the sweat you lose during exercise contains more water than salt. As your bloodstream loses more water than salt to form this sweat, the salt concentration in your bloodstream rises. In your brain are certain cells called osmoreceptors. They let you know that you are thirsty only when the salt concentration in your bloodstream rises to high levels. If sweat contained all water and no salt, the salt concentration of your bloodstream would rise very quickly as soon as you began to sweat. The more salt that passes from your bloodstream to form sweat, the longer it takes to raise the salt concentration of your blood, the more water is lost from your bloodstream in the meantime, and the longer it takes to feel thirsty. By the time you feel thirsty, you will already have lost 2 to 4 pounds of water. You can't catch up on a water deficit of that magnitude during exercise.

Prevention of Heat Exhaustion

- Make sure that you get in shape before the weather becomes hot. It takes a strong heart to pump oxygen-rich blood to your muscles and heated blood *from* your muscles to your skin.
- Take it easy on the first few days the weather suddenly turns hot. As mentioned earlier, it takes about a week for your body to acclimatize to the heat.
- On hot days, drink four ounces of water a few minutes before you start to exercise and at least every 15 minutes during exercise. You can't depend on thirst to tell you when you are dehydrated.
- If you feel weak and tired during exercise, stop exercising and drink a few ounces of water. Lack of water causes you to feel tired.
- If you continue to feel weak and tired, check with your doctor to see if you have heat exhaustion, salt deficiency, or another illness. You can also weigh yourself each morning. If you find that you are losing weight without any change in your diet or exercise pattern, chances are that you are becoming progressively dehydrated and are suffering from heat exhaustion.
- Don't take salt tablets. They can upset your stomach, dehydrate you, and even increase your chances of forming clots in your bloodstream. If you have these symptoms, a blood test can be done to determine if you lack salt.

HEATSTROKE

Heatstroke is a condition in which your body temperature rises uncontrollably and makes you pass out.

Warning Signals of Heatstroke

During exercise it is normal for body temperature to rise. Normal temperature is 98.6 degrees Fahrenheit. Temperatures of 102 to 104 degrees are to be expected during exercise. However, when your temperature rises higher than that, there is a set sequence of warning signals:

- First your muscles will start to burn. They will hurt and feel like someone is touching a hot poker against them.
- Then you will find it very difficult to breathe. The air will feel as if it is coming from a heated furnace. No matter how hard you breathe, you won't feel that you are getting enough air. An elevated body temperature increases your metabolism so much that you need more oxygen. Your temperature can rise so high that you can't get all the oxygen you need, no matter how rapidly you breathe.
- Your entire body will feel hot.
- Next, your head will start to hurt. This means that your temperature is more than 105 degrees. You had better stop exercising and get help immediately because the next series of events will occur very quickly.
- You may hear ringing in your ears and will see spots in front of your eyes. Suddenly you won't be able to see at all.
- You will then be lying on the ground unconscious, perhaps having seizures.

Mary T., a 16-year-old high school student, entered a 10-kilometer road race when the weather had just started to become warmer. She thought that she would run better if she took a stimulant, so she drank three cups of coffee three hours before the race. She drank no other fluids. She was in second place in the race until the last hundred yards. She broke into a sprint and caught the girl in front of her just before the finish line. Then she fell on the ground unconscious and went into convulsions. An alert physician immediately poured water on her from a hose. A thermometer placed in her armpit showed a temperature of 105 degrees Fahrenheit. Within five minutes, she had stopped convulsing and was alert and talking to the people around her. They stopped hosing her, and three minutes later she lay unconscious on the ground again in convulsions. The hose was turned on her immediately and within a minute she was alert and appeared fine. She had no further complications. However, her muscles were so sore that she couldn't run for more than two weeks.

Mary made several mistakes that could have killed her. She drank three cups of coffee which contained caffeine, a potent stimulant. As we discussed in Chapter 3, stimulants affect your mind, so that you are less likely to respond to the severe pain that precedes heatstroke, and you may not stop exercising. Most cases of heatstroke occur when the athlete increases the intensity of exercise, such as the final sprint to the tape. Mary also failed to heed the warning signals that are mentioned above.

Being dehydrated raises your body temperature even higher, thereby increasing your chances of developing heatstroke. So always make sure that you drink fluids frequently when you exercise in hot weather.

Treatment of Heatstroke

When a previously healthy person suddenly passes out while exercising on a warm day, she probably has heatstroke. Treatment must be started immediately because her temperature is probably greater than 106 degrees Fahrenheit and her brain is being cooked in the same way that the colorless part of an egg turns white when it hits the griddle.

Seek medical help immediately. Then move the victim into the shade so that the sun will not continue to heat her body. Strip extra clothing from her body. Place her in shock position, with her legs higher than her body. This allows gravity to help extra blood circulate to the brain. Then cool her by any means available. Hosing is probably best, but fans, ice baths, and rubbing ice on the skin will also work. If nothing else is available to pour on her, you can use water, milk, soft drinks, or anything else that is wet. The evaporation of any liquid will help to cool her body.

The victim's temperature should be closely monitored because all cooling should be stopped when her temperature drops to 101 degrees. Continued cooling can cause her body temperature to fall too low, and she can go into shock from too low a temperature.

After the cooling is stopped, the victim's temperature may rise again and she may pass out again. Therefore, all victims of heatstroke must be watched for several hours after they are revived. If they pass out again, cooling must be started again.

EXERCISE IN THE COLD

It's not just the temperature that determines how uncomfortable you will be when you exercise outside. The wind is also very important.

> On a cold winter day, we started our long Sunday run with the wind blowing firmly at our backs. We couldn't understand why the weather reporters were warning everyone to stay indoors. We felt very comfortable and were sweating profusely.
>
> When we reached the halfway point, we turned around and ran into the wind. There was a point when we actually thought we wouldn't make it. The wind caused our sweat to evaporate and made us feel cold. It also blew through our clothes and made us feel so miserable that we thought we were going to freeze to death.
>
> —Gabe Mirkin, M.D. and
> Mona Shangold, M.D.

Below is a wind-chill chart. It shows that the harder the wind blows, the colder you will feel. For example, a 20 degree day with the wind blowing 40 miles per hour will feel as if it is 20 degrees below zero.

Never underestimate the dangers of wintertime exercise. If your skin freezes, it can be damaged permanently. If you become cold enough, your body temperature can drop low enough to kill you. However, these complications should never happen to you. If you read on, you will learn how to exercise safely, even on the coldest days.

Wind-Chill Factors

WIND (MPH)	TEMPERATURE (FAHRENHEIT)																				
Calm	40°	35°	30°	25°	20°	15°	10°	5°	0°	−5°	−10°	−15°	−20°	−25°	−30°	−35°	−40°	−45°	−50°	−55°	−60°
											Equivalent Chill Temperature										
5	35°	30°	25°	20°	15°	10°	5°	0°	−5°	−10°	−15°	−20°	−25°	−30°	−35°	−40°	−45°	−50°	−55°	−65°	−70°
10	30°	20°	15°	10°	5°	0°	−10°	−15°	−20°	−25°	−35°	−40°	−45°	−50°	−60°	−65°	−70°	−75°	−80°	−90°	−95°
15	25°	15°	10°	0°	−5°	−10°	−20°	−25°	−30°	−40°	−45°	−50°	−60°	−65°	−70°	−80°	−85°	−90°	−100°	−105°	−110°
20	20°	10°	5°	0°	−10°	−15°	−25°	−30°	−35°	−45°	−50°	−60°	−65°	−75°	−80°	−85°	−95°	−100°	−110°	−115°	−120°
25	15°	10°	0°	−5°	−15°	−20°	−30°	−35°	−45°	−50°	−60°	−65°	−75°	−80°	−90°	−95°	−105°	−110°	−120°	−125°	−135°
30	10°	5°	0°	−10°	−20°	−25°	−30°	−40°	−50°	−55°	−65°	−70°	−80°	−85°	−95°	−100°	−105°	−115°	−120°	−130°	−140°
35	10°	5°	−5°	−10°	−20°	−25°	−35°	−40°	−50°	−60°	−65°	−75°	−80°	−90°	−100°	−105°	−115°	−120°	−130°	−135°	−145°
40°	10°	0°	−5°	−15°	−20°	−30°	−35°	−45°	−55°	−60°	−70°	−75°	−85°	−95°	−100°	−110°	−115°	−125°	−130°	−140°	−150°

Little danger — *Increasing danger (Flesh may freeze within one minute)* — *Great danger (Flesh may freeze within 30 seconds)*

*Winds above 40 mph have little additional effect.

On a cold winter day, you may have seen people running down the street wearing brief shorts and flimsy shirts with woolen socks, hats, and mittens. Experienced runners always wear warm woolen socks, hats, and mittens because their toes, ears, and fingers are the sites likely to feel cold first.

The feeling of being cold comes from special cold receptors in your skin. You do not feel the chill of a cold winter day from inside your body. The receptors in your skin that are most sensitive to cold are in your fingers, ears, and toes. When the outside temperature drops below 40 degrees Fahrenheit, the cold will not bother you as much if you wear a warm woolen hat, mittens, warm socks, and boots.

Dressing for the Cold

When the outside temperature is 20 degrees Fahrenheit, more than 40 percent of the heat that you lose escapes from your head. At 5 degrees Fahrenheit, more than 70 percent of the heat lost will come from your head. On cold winter days, wear a woolen hat that pulls down over your ears and covers your neck. Mittens are preferable to gloves because the fingers warm each other in the same compartment. The fingers in gloves warm individual chambers so that more heat is lost through your hands.

On very cold days, you must cover more than your fingers, ears, and toes. You must also protect your body. If you don't, you could lose so much heat that your body temperature would drop to low levels, your heart would start to beat irregularly, and you could die.

> A young couple wearing blue jeans and denim jackets were caught in a rainstorm on the Appalachian Trail. They both died of hypothermia, a low body temperature, even though the outside temperature never went below 40 degrees Fahrenheit.

Blue jeans and denim jackets are made of cotton, which loses almost all of its insulating properties when wet. The couple wearing

During World War II, American gunners complained bitterly about freezing their fingers, ears, and toes in the cold turrets of the large bombers. The gunners were then supplied with specially insulated mittens, hats, and boots. They came back frostbitten on their faces but they didn't complain about the cold. You feel cold most in your fingers, ears and toes.

wet cotton clothing had little more protection than they would have had if they had been naked.

Your clothes don't keep you warm. You keep your clothes warm. The function of clothes is to help your body retain some of the heat that you produce.

There is no need to wear heavy outer garments. Insulation is determined by the thickness of a garment, not by how much it weighs. The more you layer your clothes, the more air is trapped in each layer. Air is an excellent insulator.

The best outer layers are those that block the wind and the rain. The best materials for these are polypropylene and wool because they dry from the inside out and are good insulators, even when wet. To block the wind, all outer layers should have a very tight weave.

Both wool and polypropylene are also excellent for inner layers because they carry sweat away from your skin and keep you warm while doing so. The difference between ideal inner and outer layers is the weave: The inner layer should be loosely woven to carry sweat away from your body; the outer layer should be tightly woven to block the wind. Although silk is an excellent fabric to serve as an inner layer, it is much too expensive and difficult to clean to be practical for exercise.

Can You Acclimatize to the Cold?

Cold weather will bother you much more when you *start* to exercise in the cold. As you continue to exercise in the cold, you will be able to tolerate the cold with far less discomfort.

The exact mechanism of acclimatization to cold is not known; however, many scientists offer the following explanation based on experiments in animals. There are two types of fat in the body. The conventional yellow fat, which is located under the skin and around the organs, comprises more than 99 percent of the fat in the body. Brown fat, which is the heat-producing fat in the body, is located around the large blood vessels that carry blood back to the heart and kidneys. The main function of brown fat is to warm the blood as it returns to the heart. If cold blood enters the heart, the heart muscle can become chilled. This can lead to irregular heart beats and even death.

Repeated exposure to cold weather causes the body to produce more brown fat. The more brown fat, the more heat is produced and the better cold weather can be tolerated.

Can You Freeze Your Lungs?

It's almost impossible to damage your lungs by breathing cold air when you exercise. Air that is inhaled at −40 degrees Fahrenheit will be warmed more than 100 degrees before it reaches your lungs. Air at −40 degrees is so cold and would burn your nose, throat, and mouth so badly that only the worst masochist would think of exercising in weather that cold.

If breathing cold air when you exercise makes you uncomfortable, you can purchase a face mask that will cover your mouth and nose. An excellent one costs less than $5.00 and can be purchased at your drugstore.

Frostbite

Frostbite means that your tissue is frozen. If the weather is cold enough, you can freeze your skin, tendons, muscles, and even bones.

> Groups of people, like the Coney Island Polar Bears in New York and the L Street Brownies in Boston, get together and go swimming in the middle of the winter, even when the temperature drops below freezing.
>
> They do not develop frostbite because they get out of the water and dry themselves off immediately when their skin turns red and starts to burn and itch.

It wasn't the Russians who beat Napoleon. It was frostbite and the French surgeons. During the day, the soldiers marched in the cold and froze their fingers and toes. During the night, the French surgeons rubbed snow on the frostbitten extremities.

The fluid in and around your cells turns to ice. Then when the tissue thaws, the cells can burst and be damaged forever.

When your skin is exposed to very cold weather, its temperature starts to drop. Your body tries to conserve heat by constricting the blood vessels in your skin, turning it white. If you remain in the cold, your skin temperature will continue to drop until it reaches about 59 degrees Fahrenheit. Then your body tries to protect your skin from being damaged. The blood vessels in your skin open wide and your skin turns red and feels hot. It will itch and start to burn.

When this happens, get out of the cold. If you don't get out of the cold, the blood vessels will close down again and your skin temperature will continue to drop. When it drops below freezing, your skin will turn white and freeze.

Most of the damage from frostbite occurs when the skin is re-warmed, causing the cells to burst and be damaged forever. Most doctors recommend that the skin be warmed in water set at 102 to 104 degrees Fahrenheit. Temperatures lower than that rewarm the skin too slowly and increase the likelihood that the cells will burst. Temperatures higher than that can burn the skin and cause blisters. Needless to say, rubbing the skin with snow will remove skin and expose the fat, muscles, and tendons that are located underneath.

Hypothermia

Normal body temperature is 98.6 degrees. You have seen that temperatures much higher than that can damage your brain. Temperatures much lower than normal are also bad. They can cause your heart to stop beating, thereby preventing blood from circulating through your body.

A consistent pattern of signs will tell you if your body temperature starts to drop and approximately how low it has dropped:

On a backpacking trip, it started to rain. We didn't have adequate equipment to protect us from the rain, so we all were soaked. One of our friends started to talk with slurred speech. We tried to keep moving, but she started to stumble and couldn't walk. She sat down on a tree stump and couldn't get up.

That meant that her body temperature had dropped more than three degrees. We took off her clothes and she got into a sleeping bag with some of the other women. Their body heat rewarmed her and she eventually was able to accompany us back to shelter.

- A drop of at least one degree: You will start to shiver and your speech will become slurred.
- A drop of at least two degrees: You will find it difficult to use your fingers and control your hands.
- A drop of at least three degrees: You will start to stumble and will have difficulty walking.
- A drop of at least four degrees: Your brain is affected and you will find it difficult to think clearly.
- A drop of at least nine degrees: Shivering is replaced by muscle rigidity.

This woman could have died. She was saved by using the body heat of other people to warm her. The treatment of hypothermia is rapid rewarming. Doctors use warm baths, heating pads, heating lamps, or lots of blankets.

5 PREVENTING AND TREATING INJURIES

If you go to your doctor with a sports-related injury and your doctor gives you medicine for pain, telling you to rest and offering you nothing further, find yourself another doctor. That's like treating body odor with perfume. The treatment for sports-related injuries includes:

• Stop participating in the sport that caused the injury until you can practice that sport without pain. Pain is the message your body sends to tell you that something has been injured.
• Find another sport that causes no pain when you do it.
• Correct the cause of the injury.

Bones are the supporting structures of your body. *Muscles* contract and relax to permit movement of your bones. The word "muscle" is derived from the Latin word *musculus,* which means "little mouse." Like a mouse, a muscle has a head, a body, and a tail. Its head is its tendinous origin, its body is the fleshy middle portion (made of the muscle fibers themselves), and its tail is its tendinous insertion. Thus, each *tendon* attaches a muscle body to a bone.

Ligaments are fibrous bands that hold bones together. *Joints* are the places where two bones come together. Bones are too soft to rub against each other without wearing away. So everywhere bones come together, their ends are protected by a hard white gristle called *cartilage.*

SUDDEN AND GRADUAL INJURIES

Some injuries occur suddenly as a result of trauma; these are called *acute*. Others occur gradually as a result of repeated wear-and-tear; these are called *chronic*. Acute and chronic injuries must be treated differently.

The immediate treatment for almost all sudden athletic injuries is RICE, a mnemonic composed of the first letters of a four-part treatment.

1. **Rest:** Stop exercising immediately when you first feel pain. When tissue is injured, there is bleeding and tearing. If you continue to exercise, you will cause further bleeding and tearing.
2. **Ice:** The application of cold contricts the blood vessels in your skin and limits swelling. The greater the swelling, the longer it takes for tissue to heal, and vice versa.
3. **Compression:** Wrapping something around the injured part can help to limit swelling.
4. **Elevation:** Elevating the injured part above the level of your heart uses gravity to drain fluid from the injured part and helps to limit swelling.

You need to do all of these things only if you have suffered a sudden injury in which you have severe pain. If you develop a wear-and-tear injury in which you gradually develop a pain while exercising, you only need to rest.

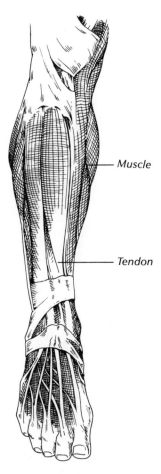

Muscle

Tendon

Figure 5-1. Muscle and Tendon.

SUDDEN SEVERE INJURY

When you develop a sudden, severe injury, such as by twisting your ankle, stepping in a hole, falling on a ski slope, or getting hit with a baseball, stop exercising and elevate the injured part above the level of your heart. If your leg is injured, lie down and prop up your leg on several pillows. If your arm is injured, prop up your arm on pillows. Then place a towel on the skin over your injured part. On top of the towel place an ice bag or a special bag that becomes cold when a chemical is released into it. You can buy chemical cold bags at many sport stores.

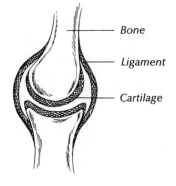

Bone

Ligament

Cartilage

Figure 5-2. Joint with Ligament and Cartilage.

Next take a strip of cloth and wrap it loosely over the ice bag and around the injured part. Make sure that the wrapping is loose enough so that you do not block the flow of blood. Do not wrap anything around your neck (or anyone's), for it may interfere with breathing.

Do not leave the compression-ice bandage on for more than 15 minutes. If you leave the ice in place for longer than that, the swelling may increase instead of decreasing. When you place ice on the skin, the temperature of the skin drops. Then, as the temperature drops closer to freezing, your body makes an effort to warm the skin by opening the blood vessels. The skin turns red and swells and starts to burn and hurt. Correct treatment is to remove the ice before this happens.

Leave the ice off the injury for at least fifteen minutes and repeat the treatment once or twice. Then follow the rules in the next section to help you return to your exercise program.

WEAR-AND-TEAR INJURY

If you develop an injury in which you were not hit, tackled or otherwise physically traumatized, you probably have a wear-and-tear injury. This may be caused by poor training methods, weak tissue, or a biomechanical weakness in your body.

The Linked Chain

If a chain is pulled hard enough, it will break at its weakest link. If the chain is repaired and then again pulled hard enough, it will break again at the same spot, which is still its weakest link.

The same principle applies to your body. You may go out and start a running program, run three miles a week and do fine. As you get into shape, you are able to run more miles. You work up to 10, then 20 miles. Then when you reach 30 miles a week, you pull your hamstring muscle, or develop pain in your knee or heel. You then rest and heal. You start to run again, and when you build up to 30 miles a week again, you develop the same injury.

Stop Participating in the Same Sport

When you are injured in a sport, stop playing that sport until you can do it without feeling pain. If you continue to play that sport with pain, you will stress the injured body part and delay healing.

Your muscles, tendons, and ligaments are made up of thousands of string-like fibers in the same way that a rope is made up of many threads. Muscles, tendons, and ligaments are injured when fibers are torn. Pain means that some fibers are torn and, because of this, there are fewer fibers to do their job of moving the parts of your body or holding the parts of your body together. So, during exercise, greater force is placed on the remaining fibers, and more fibers are likely to tear.

Pain in a bone usually means that there is a small crack or a break in the surface. Continuing to stress an injured bone can extend the break.

Find Another Sport That Doesn't Hurt

When you stop exercising, your muscles will immediately start to shrink, and you will have less strength and endurance. For every week you rest, it will usually take you at least two weeks of exercising to get back to the level of fitness you enjoyed at the time you were injured. Therefore, you should not stop exercising altogether. You should find a sport that causes no pain.

Your muscles become smaller and weaker when you stop exercising because exercise is the main stimulus to build and maintain muscle. The protein in your muscles is made up of basic building blocks called amino acids. Enzymes, as defined in Chapter 2, are chemicals that make reactions happen in your body. Some enzymes break down muscle protein and release the amino acids into the bloodstream. Other enzymes cause amino acids to go from the bloodstream into the muscle. Exercise increases the number of enzymes that stimulate muscle growth and endurance. It does not increase the number of degrading enzymes significantly. When you stop exercising, the number of building enzymes decreases and the muscles become smaller and weaker.

Which Alternate Sport Do You Choose?

Different sports stress different parts of your body. For example, running stresses primarily your lower leg. You run by landing on your heel and coming up on your toes. You raise your body up by using the calf muscles in your lower leg.

ALTERNATE SPORTS FOLLOWING AN INJURY

Lower leg and foot injuries
Bicycling
Swimming
Skating
Skiing
Pulling on a rowing machine

Upper leg injuries
Jogging in place
Jogging on a trampoline
Swimming
Rowing

Lower back injuries
Bicycling
Swimming

Shoulder and arm injuries
Jogging
Skating
Skiing

Bicycling stresses primarily your upper leg. So do skiing and skating. You pedal with your hips and knees. You ski and skate by bouncing up and down on your hips and knees. You swim primarily with your arms and shoulders.

If you injure your lower leg in running, you may still be able to ride a bicycle. If you injure your upper leg, you can usually swim or jog in place. You use the hamstrings in the back of your upper leg primarily to drive you forward when you run.

If you injure your back, you can usually ride a bicycle. You do not use your back muscles to pedal.

Correcting the Cause

Every wear-and-tear injury is caused by a force on a tissue that is greater than the tissue's inherent strength. Either the tissue is too weak or the force is too great. We have devised the following classification of causes:

- Poor training methods that do not allow for adequate recovery
- Weak tissues that are more likely to be broken or torn
- Biomechanical factors that put excessive stress on certain parts of your body

Poor Training Methods

You improve your athletic skill by stressing your body. You recover from each stress by resting it. You won't become a better athlete by doing the same workout every day. For example, if you want to run faster, you must run very fast in practice. If you want to have greater endurance, you must run longer distances. You can't stress your body every day because it needs at least 48 hours to recover after each intense workout.

Each muscle is made up of thousands of stringy fibers. Every time you stress your body, some of your fibers are injured and some use up all of their stored sugar. It takes at least 48 hours for them to heal, and it can take even longer for the fibers to refill with sugar.

The main energy source for your muscles is the sugar that is stored in them. On the day after a hard workout, some fibers will refill with sugar, while others will not. Only the fibers that have the stored sugar in them will be able to contract and function properly. The fibers that lack stored sugar will not contract. If you work out at the same level the next day, your muscles will have to do the same job with fewer functioning fibers. This means that a greater stress will be placed on the fibers that are still functioning and they will be more likely to tear.

That's why most training methods in almost every sport emphasize the hard-easy principle. You exercise intensely on one day and at a more relaxed pace on the next. (See Chapter 1.)

If you are a weight lifter, you do your hard workout one day and you don't even try to lift weights on the next. If you are a runner, you may run at a six-minute pace on one day and an eight-minute pace on the next.

Weak Tissue

Muscles, tendons, and ligaments can be injured because they are not strong enough to withstand the forces that are transmitted to them. Prevention of injuries to these tissues involves strengthening by appropriate resistance exercises. Bones can be weakened by lack of calcium, resistance exercise, or estrogen. To prevent bone injuries, you must treat the cause. Joints are more likely to become damaged when the supporting structures around the joint, such as muscles, tendons, and ligaments, are weak. This allows the bones to move freely about the joint, causing the cartilages covering the ends of the bones to rub against each other. To prevent joint injuries, you must strengthen the supporting structures.

Rehabilitating Injured Tissue

You rehabilitate injured tissue by exercising against resistance in three sets of 10, every other day.

Exercise strengthens your muscles only if it is done against resistance. As we discussed in Chapter 1, strength training is usually done in sets of 10, to increase the number of muscle fibers that are being strengthened. Since you are strengthening tissue that was injured previously, you shouldn't even *try* to lift very heavy weights. That would only increase your chances of reinjuring the tissue. Lifting lighter weights won't provide enough resistance to strengthen weakened muscles. So you have to do more sets. Most rehabilitation is done in three sets of 10 repetitions, with a minute's rest between each set.

If you have a pulled muscle, you will go to your trainer, doctor, or physical therapist and learn which muscle is injured and what its function is. Then you should strengthen the injured muscle in its functional position, provided that it doesn't hurt to do this. If it hurts, you're not rehabilitating your muscle, you're reinjuring it. More information about rehabilitation will be given when we discuss specific treatments later in this chapter.

Biomechanical Factors

Certain structural abnormalities can stress certain parts of your body excessively. Having a deep curve in your lower back increases your chances of developing back pain. The bones of your spine form a forward curve, rather than sitting one on top of the other. This places excessive force on the muscles and ligaments that support the spinal bones and keep them from curving forward even more.

If one leg is longer than the other, a greater force is placed on the hip and knees of the longer leg. Many roads are slanted about two degrees toward the sides to facilitate drainage. If you always run on roads rather than sidewalks, and always run against traffic, your right leg will always be hitting ground higher than your left. This increases your chances of developing pain in your right hip.

By far the most common biomechanical factor that causes injury is improper rolling of the foot after it strikes the ground.

Pronation and Supination

One of the most important biomechanical causes of wear-and-tear sports injuries is excessive pronation. When you run, you land on the outside (lateral) bottom side of your foot and you roll toward the inside (medial). This is called *pronation* and is good because it helps to protect you from developing injuries. During running, your foot strikes the ground with a force that can equal three times your body weight. Pronation helps to distribute the force of your footstrike throughout your entire leg rather than letting this force be concentrated at your knees, hips, and back.

After you pronate, you roll back toward the outer (lateral) part of the bottom of your foot. This is called *supination*. Then you raise yourself up on your toes and step off to land on your other foot.

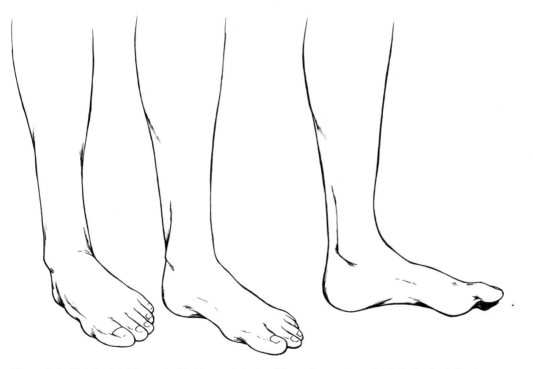

Figure 5-3. Flat-Arched Foot *(left)*, Normal-Arched Foot *(center)*, and High-Arched Foot *(right)*.

Flat Feet

People who appear to have flat feet usually have normal arches. Their feet appear to be flat because they roll in so far during walking and running that their arches roll underneath their feet and touch the ground. You can't see their arches because they are hidden under their feet. On rare occasions, people can be born with true flat feet, having no arches. Such people usually require surgical correction or special shoes.

Pronation causes your lower leg to twist inward. Try it yourself. Place the outside (lateral) side of the bottom of your foot on the ground and then roll your foot inward (medially). Observe that your lower leg twists inward.

Flat feet roll in excessively, causing increased inward twisting, which can cause foot, leg, and knee pain.

High-Arched Feet

People who appear to have high-arched feet usually have normal arches. Their arches appear to be high because they were born with such rigid ankles that their feet can barely roll inward. Their feet usually are poor shock absorbers, increasing their chances of developing small cracks in the bones of their feet and legs.

COMMON INJURIES

Many different injuries can cause pain in the same parts of your body. Different injuries often require different treatments. This section is intended only to help you understand the rules for treating injuries. It is not intended to substitute for a consultation with your physician, osteopath, podiatrist, or physical therapist.

Plantar Fasciitis

Pain on the bottom of your heel is usually *plantar fasciitis.* (It can also be bursitis, a pinched nerve, a break in the heel bone, or even a tumor.) Heel pain caused by plantar fasciitis usually hurts more when you rise onto your toes. The *plantar fascia* is a band made of tough connective tissue that supports the bottom of your foot. It starts at the base of your five toes, runs backward along the bottom of your foot,

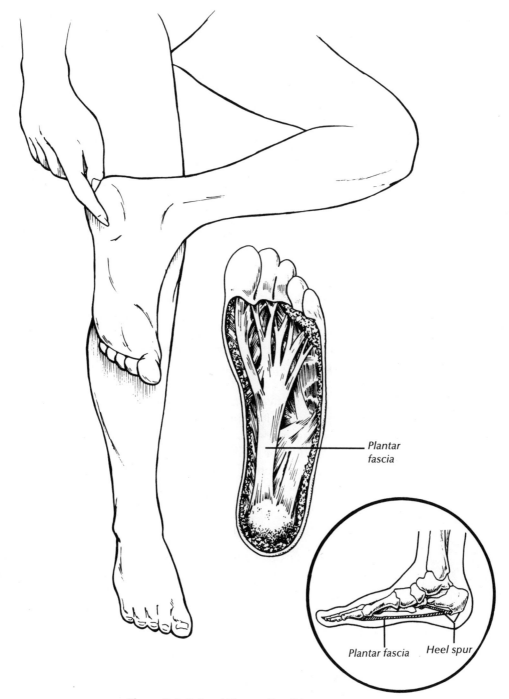

Plantar
fascia

Plantar fascia   Heel spur

Figure 5-4. Pain of Plantar Fasciitis.

and attaches on a spot on the middle bottom of your heel bone. The pain is usually due to a tearing away of the band where it attaches on the heel. Although many people have heel bone spurs where the plantar fascia attaches, these spurs do not contribute to the pain. To treat plantar fasciitis, you must stop running and reduce your walking so that the band can heal itself.

If you develop plantar fasciitis, you should do the following:

- Stop all sports that require running. Running puts great force on the plantar fascia.
- Try alternate sports, such as cycling and swimming. They stress the plantar fascia minimally.
- Wear special arch supports in low-heeled laced shoes. Pronation causes the toes to move forward and stretch the plantar fascia. Limiting pronation by using arch supports restricts the forward motion of the toes and takes some of the tension off the plantar fascia.
- Make sure that your shoes have a flexible sole that bends just behind the big toe. When you run, you land on your heel. Then you step up on your toes. If the sole is very stiff or tends to bend in an area that is different from the place where your foot bends, extra force is placed on the plantar fascia and it can tear.
- Stretch your calf muscle. The calf muscle is really an extension of the plantar fascia. Stretching the calf muscle makes that muscle more flexible, lessening the forces on the plantar fascia.
- If the pain persists, see a podiatrist, physical therapist, trainer, or orthopedist for special taping, called a low-dye strap, which can be put on your foot and will take over some of the function of your plantar fascia.

Stress Fracture of the Small Foot Bones

Stress fractures of your feet are small cracks in the surface of the bones. The most common site is the bone just behind the fourth toe. Stress fractures are caused by the cumulative force of your foot striking the ground thousands of times during running, without having the force dissipated adequately by the process of foot pronation. As already mentioned, people with rigid ankles and high-arched feet are particularly susceptible to this injury.

When you develop a stress fracture in one of the small bones of your foot, you may not realize that you've broken a bone because the

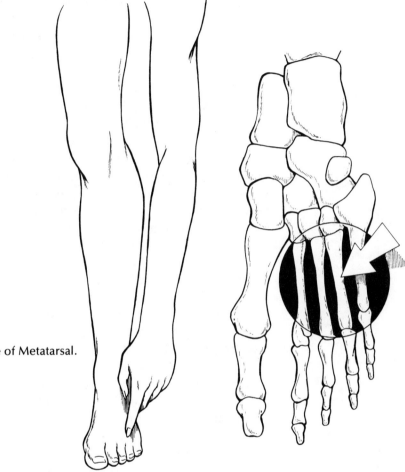

Figure 5-5. Stress Fracture of Metatarsal.

symptoms seem so mild and gradual. Typically, a stress fracture in your foot will lead to a slight pain in the front part of your foot after you have run for several minutes. The pain is not severe, so you finish your workout. After you finish the pain disappears. On the next day, you develop the same pain earlier in your run, but as you continue to run, the pain becomes so severe that you have to stop running. Again, the pain goes away after you stop running. On the next day, you develop pain as soon as you start to run. You may try to run through the pain, but you can't. When you stop running, the pain does not go away and your foot hurts all the time and is much worse with each step that you take.

You may suspect that you have a stress fracture when a single spot on top of your foot hurts when you press it with your finger. X-rays are not sensitive enough to diagnose stress fractures early. However, after you have had the pain for a month, a layer of bone, called a callus, forms over the crack. The callus can be seen on an x-ray.

Stress fractures of the feet usually occur when you increase your workload suddenly, such as running more miles or running faster. People who have high-arched feet are most likely to develop stress fractures.

As we have discussed, pronation serves as a shock-absorbing mechanism to help protect your feet from the repeated force of striking the ground. People who have high arches usually have very rigid ankles that do not allow the foot to roll in normally. Their feet strike the ground on the outside bottom part of the foot and roll in very little. The force of their footstrike is concentrated on the bones of the feet and can break them.

Since the crack in stress fractures does not extend all the way through the bone, a cast is rarely needed. These cracks usually heal by themselves within six weeks to six months.

Treatment for people with high arches and stress fractures in their feet includes reducing the force on their feet when they strike the ground. Run on grass rather than concrete, and wear sports shoes that have extra cushioning. Many manufacturers produce running shoes designed for heavier runners and those who have high arches. These shoes have extra shock-absorbing material in the soles and heels.

If you do not menstruate and have a low estrogen level, you are more susceptible to developing bones that are weak and more likely to be broken. You need a thorough evaluation for your menstrual problem, as we discuss in Chapter 6. You probably need estrogen pills to replace what your body isn't making. You also need adequate amounts of calcium in your diet. Both estrogen and calcium are necessary to protect your bones. So stress fractures should be treated as follows:

- Stop all running.
- Ride a bicycle or swim.
- Wear shoes with good cushioning.
- If you have irregular periods or amenorrhea, check with your gynecologist.
- Make sure that you eat foods or take pills totalling 1,000 milligrams of calcium a day. (See Chapter 9, Tables 9-1 and 9-2.)

Shin Splints

The term shin splints refers to pain in the lower leg, and such pain is referred to by many different names. We propose our own classification of shin splints for simplicity. These different types of lower leg pain are very common. Each is characterized by the location of the pain.

Pain on the front outside (lateral) is called "anterior shin splints" and is due to an injury to the muscles that elevate the front of your foot. Pain on the front inside (medial) is usually due to a stress fracture of your tibia (the inner bone of your lower leg). Some doctors feel that the pain is due to a tearing away of attachments on the bone, and they call it periostitis. Regardless of the cause, the treatment is the same and you can tell that you have this condition because it will hurt to press on the damaged bone. When the pain is on the rear inside (medial), the condition is called "posterior shin splints," and this involves the muscles that supinate your foot (roll it to the outside).

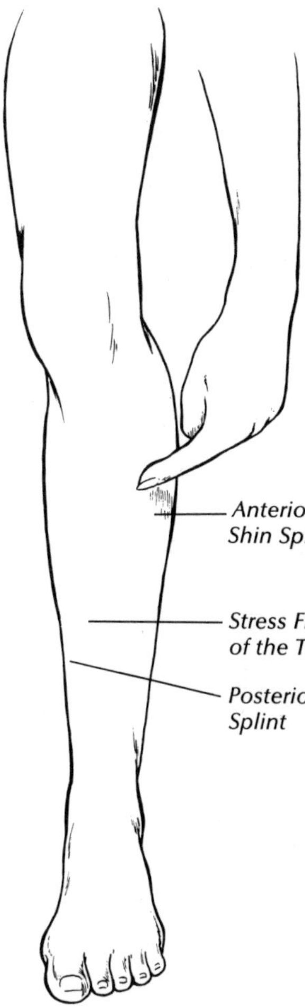

Anterior Shin Splints

Pain on the outside front of the lower leg is usually due to an injured muscle in that area. This group of muscles pulls up the front part of your foot. The larger calf muscles in the back of your lower leg pull the front part of your foot down. These muscles are often so much stronger than the shin muscles in the front of your lower leg that they can damage the weaker and smaller shin muscles opposing them.

Treatment includes resting the injured muscles and then strengthening them after they start to heal. If you have anterior shin splints, you should do the following.

- Stop running.
- Try riding a bicycle or swimming.
- Do the bucket-handle exercise (Fig. 5-7) in three sets of 10, every other day.

Anterior Shin Splint

Stress Fracture of the Tibia

Posterior Shin Splint

Figure 5-6. Shin Splints.

Stress Fracture of the Tibia

If touching the hard bone on the inside part of your lower leg causes pain, you probably have a stress fracture of this bone (the tibia). The bone may have been broken by an imbalance between your

Figure 5-7. Bucket Handle Exercise.

1. Wrap a towel around the handle of a water bucket.
2. Sit on a table that is high enough to let your feet dangle without touching the ground.
3. Place the bucket handle over the front part of your shoe.
4. Slowly raise the front part of your foot by bending your ankle. Then slowly lower it. Do this 10 times, rest a minute and do two more sets of 10.
5. As you get stronger, the bucket will feel lighter. To increase the resistance, add water to the bucket. Do not add so much water that it hurts to do this exercise.

shins and your calves, causing your tibia to bend in the middle. The pain can also be caused by a tearing away of the muscles and tendons where they attach on the bone. The treatment is exactly the same as for anterior shin splints. It will take from six weeks to many months to heal.

Posterior Shin Splints

Pain on the soft tissue behind the bone on the inside (medial) part of your lower leg is usually due to damage to the muscles in that location. These muscles help to raise you up on your toes and to supinate your foot after you have pronated it. The people most likely to develop posterior shin splints are those with flat feet. As we mentioned earlier, people with flat feet usually pronate (roll in) excessively. Since the insides of their feet drop lower, it takes more force to raise their feet up before toeing off, causing excessive strain on the posterior tibial muscles.

If you have posterior shin splints, you should do the following:

• Stop running until you can run without pain.
• Ride a bicycle or swim.

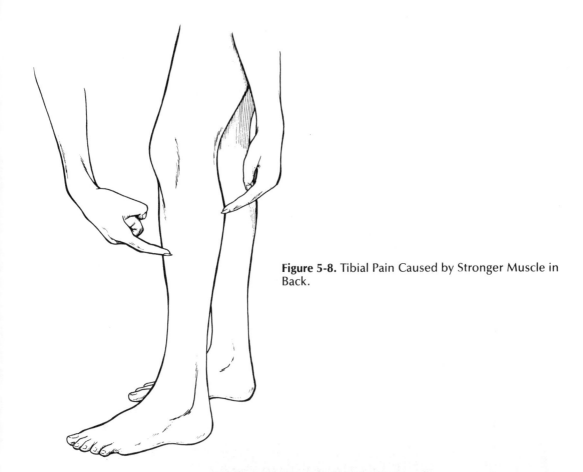

Figure 5-8. Tibial Pain Caused by Stronger Muscle in Back.

Toe Raises

Stand up. Slowly raise yourself up on your toes. Then slowly lower yourself back on your heels. Do this 10 times, rest a minute, and then do two more sets of 10. When this exercise feels easy to you, start holding progressively heavier weights in your hands.

Outward Rolls

Stand up. Slowly roll your ankles so that you raise the inside (medial) part of the bottom of your foot off the ground. Slowly lower the medial part of your foot to touch the ground again. Do three sets of 10.

- Wear special arch supports in your shoes to limit pronation.
- Strengthen the injured muscles with special exercises.

Achilles Tendinitis

Your Achilles tendon originates in your calf muscle and goes along the back of your lower leg to attach to the sides and bottom of your heel. During running, you usually land on your heel. It is your calf muscle that raises you up onto your toes as you step off to land on your other foot. *Achilles tendinitis* is an inflammation (irritation) of your Achilles tendon. When you have Achilles tendinitis, you can feel pain anywhere in the tendon. It will hurt most when you first get up in the morning and often feels better as you continue to walk. Likewise, it hurts most when you start to exercise and often feels better as you continue to exercise.

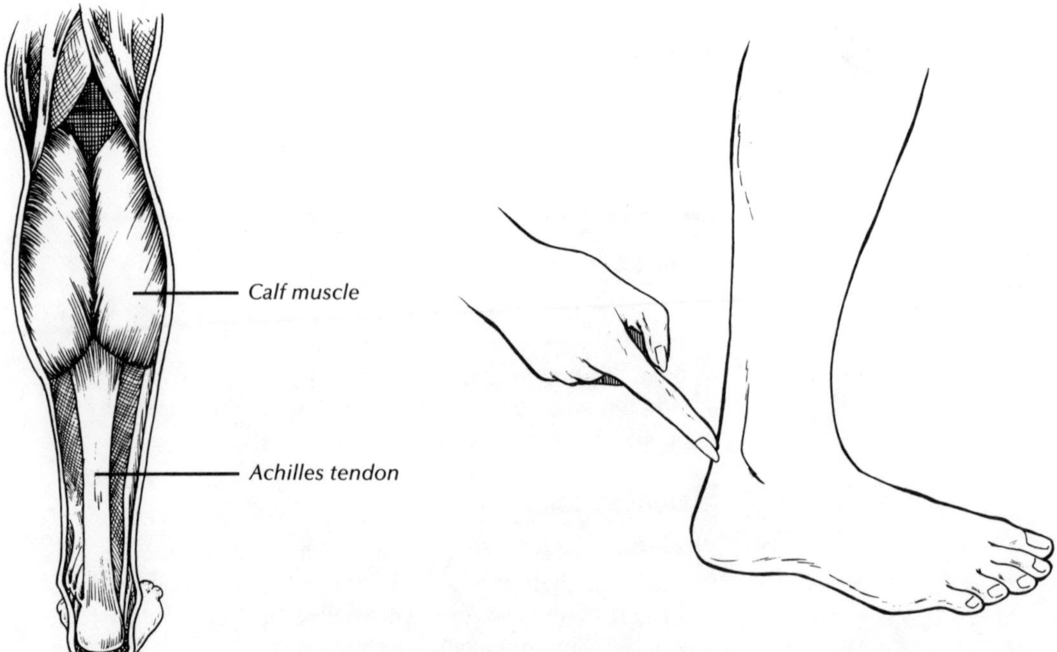

Calf muscle

Achilles tendon

Figure 5-9. Calf Muscle and Achilles Tendon.

Your tendon hurts because the individual fibers that make it up were damaged when the force on them was greater than their inherent strength. You are more likely to develop Achilles tendinitis if you have tight tendons. Stretching can help to prevent this condition, but you should not stretch your Achilles tendon when it hurts, as doing so will worsen the irritation and pain.

If you have Achilles tendinitis, you should do the following:

- Stop running.
- Avoid stretching your Achilles tendon.
- Try cycling or swimming.
- Strengthen your Achilles tendon:
  1. Stand up.
  2. Raise yourself up onto your toes. Do three sets of 10.
  3. When you can do this without too much pain, start holding weights in your hands. Keep adding as much weight as you can comfortably.

Runner's Knee

Runner's knee is a condition in which you have pain in your kneecap. The back of your kneecap fits into a groove in the lower part of your femur, the long bone of your thigh. When you run, your kneecap is supposed to move up and down in that groove without rubbing against your femur. Sometimes the kneecap moves to the side and rubs against the femur, and this causes pain.

Several different structural factors can cause the back of your kneecap to rub against your femur:

1. You may have a very shallow groove in your femur. Therefore, your kneecap may sit in front or on top of the groove rather than in it. This allows your kneecap to move toward the outside (laterally) and rub against the side of the groove.
2. You may have a kneecap that sits so high above the groove that it slips sideways.
3. You may have bands underneath your kneecap. During running, your kneecap can rub against these bands and hurt.
4. The most common cause of runner's knee is a combination of excessive pronation (inward rolling) of the foot and excessive pulling of the kneecap toward the outside (laterally). This results primarily from a muscle imbalance in your quadriceps, the large muscle group in front of your thigh.

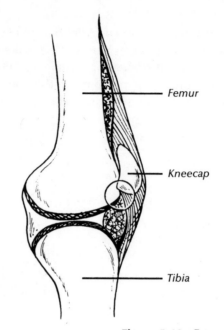

Figure 5-10. Runner's Knee with Kneecap in Groove. Flat foot causes the lower leg to twist inward, which, in turn, causes the kneecap to rub against the long bone of the thigh.

During pronation, your lower leg twists inward. At the same time, your kneecap is pulled in the opposite direction. Your kneecap is controlled by your quadriceps muscles, four muscles that are located on the front of your thigh. Three of these muscles pull your kneecap toward the outside (laterally). Only one, your vastus medialis, pulls your kneecap inward (medially). The three lateral-pulling muscles are usually more powerful than the single medial-pulling muscle. So your kneecap moves laterally. This causes the back of your kneecap to rub against the outside (lateral) groove of your femur.

Treatment for runner's knee includes:

Figure 5-11.
Runner's Knee
(pain in kneecap).

- Stop running until you can run without pain.
- Ride a bicycle if it doesn't hurt to pedal. If it hurts, pull on a rowing machine or swim.
- Place special inserts in both your walking and your exercise shoes. The inserts should be built up under the arches so that they limit pronation. You can buy these for less than $15 in many stores that

carry athletic shoes. The inserts will limit pronation only if you use them in low-heeled shoes with laces and a stiff heel counter to keep you from rolling over the insert.

- Do exercises to strengthen your vastus medialis (Figs. 5-12 and 5-13), which pulls your kneecap toward the inside (medially).

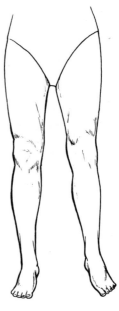

Figure 5-12. Exercise to Strengthen Vastus Medialis. Note that right knee is locked.

Stand up with your knee straight. Contract your quadriceps by locking your knee. This raises your kneecap. Hold this position for a count of 10 and then relax. Do this exercise frequently throughout the day.

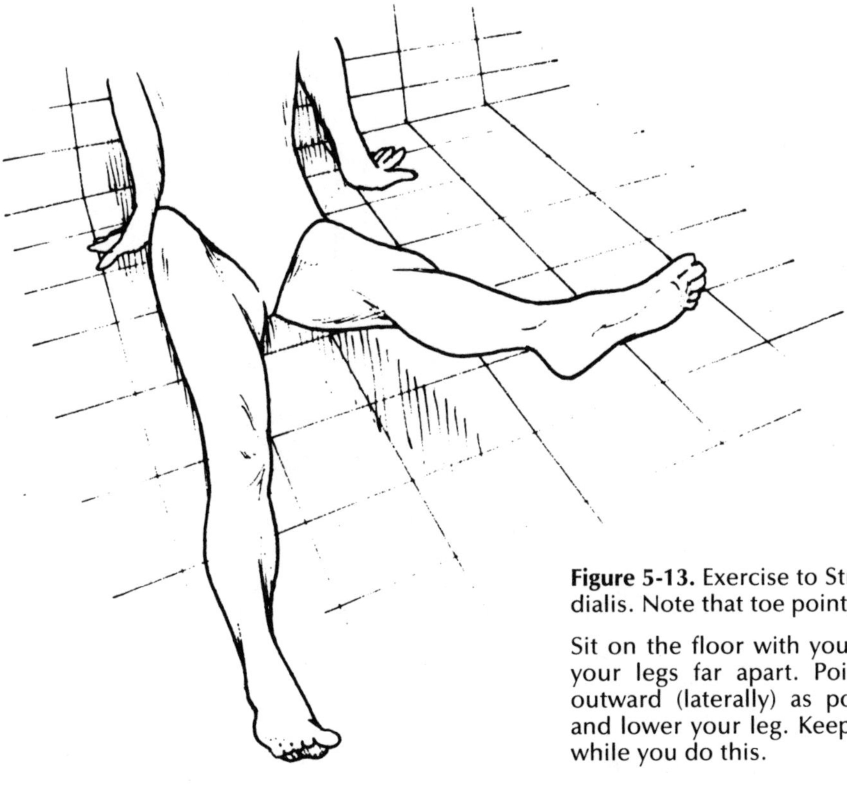

Figure 5-13. Exercise to Strengthen Vastus Medialis. Note that toe points outward.

Sit on the floor with your knees straight and your legs far apart. Point your toes as far outward (laterally) as possible. Slowly raise and lower your leg. Keep your knees straight while you do this.

Hamstring Pull

Your hamstrings are the huge muscles in the back of your thighs. Each is a two-joint muscle, moving your thigh backward from your hip and your lower leg backward from your knee.

When you tear your hamstring, you will feel pain in the back of your upper leg. This can happen with a sudden pull while sprinting or with a gradual pull while running a long distance. Usually, your injured hamstring will hurt when you run or when you squeeze it with your hand.

If you have a torn hamstring muscle, you should do the following:

- Stop running.
- Try jogging in place, rowing, or swimming. But don't do these sports if they cause pain.
- Strengthen the injured muscles after they have started to heal.

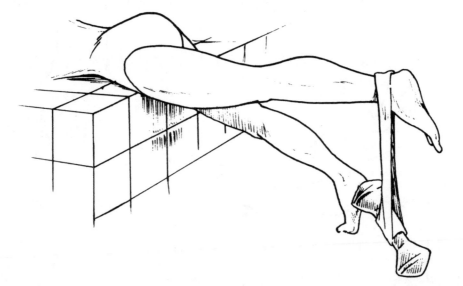

Figure 5-14. Exercises to Strengthen the Hamstrings (*above*, after high hamstring tear; *facing page*, after low hamstring tear).

To strengthen your hamstrings, primarily the top (after a high hamstring tear):

1. Attach a five-pound weight to your foot.
2. Lie face-down on a bed with your upper body on the bed and your lower body, from your waist down, off the bed. Your toes should touch the floor.
3. Keeping your knee straight, slowly raise and lower your leg. Do three sets of 10 every other day. As you become stronger, use heavier weights.

*To strengthen your hamstrings, primarily
the bottom (after a low hamstring tear):*

1. Attach a five-pound weight to your
   foot on the injured side. Stand up on
   the other foot.
2. Slowly raise your foot toward your
   buttocks by bending your knee and
   then lower it toward the floor by
   straightening your knee. Do three
   sets of 10 every other day. Increase
   the weight as you can.

Lower Back Pain

At some time in their lives, 85 percent of all women will have lower
back pain. If you do, check with your physician. You may have a
serious problem, such as a crushed disk, a broken bone in your back,
a bone out of place, or a tumor. However, 98 percent of the time a
complete medical examination will reveal only that you have strained
the muscles and ligaments that support the bones of your back or that
you have a facet syndrome—a condition in which the pain is due to
arthritis of the joints where your spinal bones come together.

When lower back pain is severe, you should rest. When you feel
well enough to start a rehabilitation program, you should check back
with your doctor.

Most lower back pain is caused by weak or inflexible back muscles. Some women have excessive curvature of the lower back, and

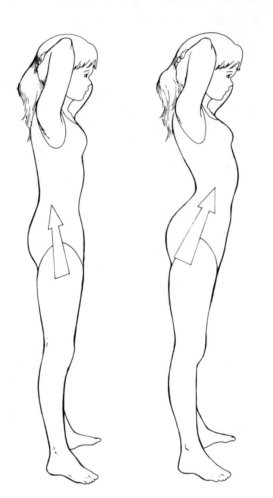

Figure 5-15.
The Normally Curved Back
and the
Deeply Curved Back.

others have rigid, inflexible backs. Certain exercises will help those with deep curves in their backs; other exercises will help those with rigid backs, and several exercises will help both groups.

Most people with lower back pain will benefit from exercises to strengthen their belly muscles and to stretch and strengthen their back muscles. In our opinion, the best way to strengthen your back muscles is by using a rowing machine.

As a general rule, if you have a deep curve in your lower back, you need special exercises to flatten your back. A deep curve in your lower back places tremendous pressure on the muscles and ligaments that support your back. As a result, these muscles and ligaments have to work harder to keep your back from curving forward even further.

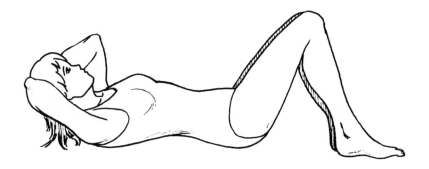

Figure 5-16.
Belly Strengthening Exercise.

1. Lie on your back with your knees bent.
2. Put your hands behind your neck.
3. While keeping your shoulders on the ground, slowly raise your head.
4. Slowly raise your shoulders off the ground about 10 inches and then slowly lower yourself.
5. Do three sets of 10.
6. When this exercise becomes too easy, wrap a weight in a towel and hold it behind your neck. Increase the weight as you become stronger.

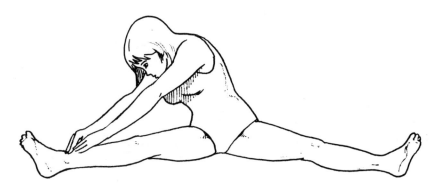

Figure 5-17. Back Stretching Exercise.

1. Sit on the floor with your knees straight and your legs as far apart as possible.
2. Place both hands on the same knee.
3. Slowly move both hands down that leg toward your ankle. Stop if it hurts and do not go farther than a position that you can hold comfortably for 10 seconds.
4. Slowly release and do the other leg. Repeat 10 times.

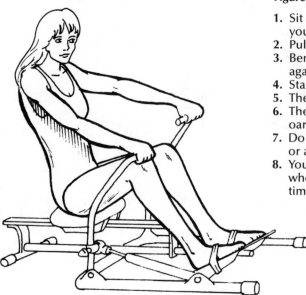

Figure 5-18. Rowing Machine.

1. Sit down on the rowing machine and place your feet in the stirrups.
2. Pull the seat as far forward as you can.
3. Bend forward and hold the oars tightly against your chest.
4. Start to row by kicking the seat backwards.
5. Then move your back backward.
6. The last part of the motion is to pull the oars with your arms.
7. Do this every other day until you feel pain or are tired.
8. You should gradually work up to the point where you can do this for 30 minutes three times a week.

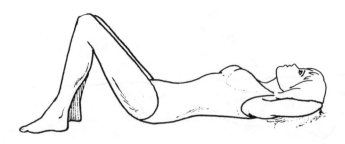

Figure 5-19. The Pelvic Tilt.

1. Lie on your back with your knees bent.
2. Lower the small of your back so that it touches the ground.
3. Put your weight on your heels.
4. Raise your pelvis about a half-inch off the ground, keeping the small of your back on the ground.
5. Contract your belly muscles.
6. Hold this position for a count of 10 and repeat 20 times. Do this daily.

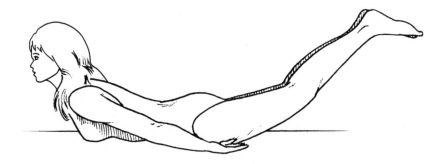

Figure 5-20. The Swan.
(*Caution.* This is a potentially dangerous exercise because it forces your spinal bones closer together and can pinch a nerve lying between them. It should not be done unless it is recommended by your physician.)

1. Lie on your belly with your arms extended alongside your torso.
2. Raise your shoulders and legs off the ground at the same time. Do not bend your knees. Stop immediately if you have pain.
3. Hold this position for a count of 10 and repeat 20 times. Do this daily.

If you have a rigid, inflexible back, you need exercises to make your back more flexible. You also need exercises to strengthen your back.

The curve in your lower back is dependent upon the tilt of your pelvis. If you have a deep curve in your back, tilting the top of your pelvis backward will decrease this curve, reducing the stress placed on your back muscles and ligaments. If you have a rigid, inflexible back, you will need special back exercises to loosen the muscles that hold the bones of your back together.

If you have a deep curve in your lower back, you should do exercises to strengthen your belly muscles, do exercises to stretch and strengthen your back muscles, use a rowing machine, and do the "pelvic tilt."

If you have a rigid, inflexible back, you should do exercises to strengthen your belly muscles (Fig. 5-16), do exercises to stretch and strengthen your back muscles (Fig. 5-17), use a rowing machine (Fig. 5-18), and do specific back flexibility exercises (Figs. 5-19 and 5-20).

Tennis Elbow

Tennis elbow is an injury in which you have torn the tendons of your forearm where they attach to your elbow. When you have this condition, it hurts to move your wrist. You don't have to play tennis to get tennis elbow. You can damage your tendons by opening a jar, pitching a baseball, bowling a ball, or pulling on a stuck door. We have both had tennis elbow from lifting or carrying heavy luggage.

If you have a pain about your elbow, check with your doctor. You may have a damaged joint, a pinched nerve, or a torn ligament. You can tell when you have tennis elbow because it will hurt to bend or straighten your wrist against resistance.

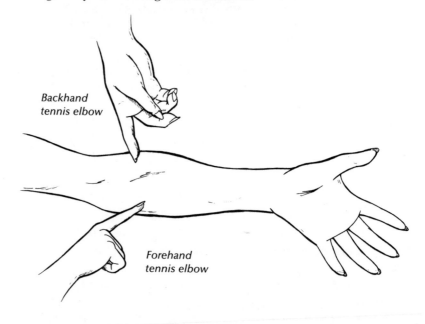

Backhand tennis elbow

Forehand tennis elbow

Figure 5-21. Types of Tennis Elbow.

Stand up with your arm by your side, your elbow straight, and your thumb pointed outward (laterally). If the pain is on the inside (medially), you probably have forehand tennis elbow, damage to the tendons that help to bend your wrist. These are the ones you use in your forehand shot. If it hurts on the outside (laterally), you probably have backhand tennis elbow, damage to the tendons that straighten your wrist (bend it backward). These are the ones you use in your backhand shot.

Figure 5-22. Exercise to Treat Backhand Tennis Elbow.

1. Sit on a chair next to a table.
2. Place your forearm on the table, palm facing **down,** with your wrist and hand hanging over the edge.
3. Hold a one-pound weight in your hand.
4. Slowly raise and lower your hand by bending and straightening your wrist.
5. Do this exercise 10 times, rest a minute, and do two more sets of 10. Stop immediately if you feel pain. Try again the next day.
6. As the exercise becomes easier for you, increase the weight that you hold in your hand.

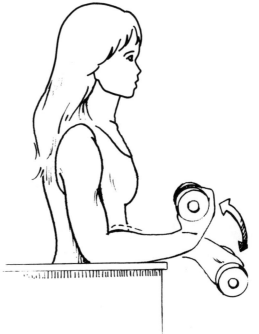

Figure 5-23. Exercise to Treat Forehand Tennis Elbow.

1. Sit on a chair next to a table.
2. Place your forearm on the table, palm facing **up,** with your wrist and hand hanging over the edge.
3. Hold a one-pound weight in your hand.
4. Slowly raise and lower your hand by bending and straightening your wrist.
5. Do this exercise 10 times, rest a minute, and do two more sets of 10. Stop immediately if you feel pain. Try again the next day.
6. As the exercise becomes easier for you, increase the weight that you hold in your hand.

Sit on a chair next to a table. Place your elbow and forearm on the table. Make a fist and point your palm downward. Have someone try to hold your hand down by placing a hand on your hand. Try to raise your hand by bending your wrist backward and upward. Pain in your elbow means that you probably have backhand tennis elbow. Next, do the same test with your palm up. If it hurts to raise your hand by bending your wrist, you probably have forehand tennis elbow.

You tore the tendons because the force on them was greater than their inherent strength. The treatment is to strengthen the tendons, as soon as they have started to heal.

If you have tennis elbow, you should do the following:

- Stop playing tennis or doing any other activity that causes pain.
- Try jogging, cycling, basketball, or anything else that doesn't cause pain.
- Do the exercises to treat backhand tennis elbow (Fig. 5-22) or forehand tennis elbow (Fig. 5-23) every other day.

6 MENSTRUATION

HOW DO WOMEN FEEL ABOUT MENSTRUATION?

All women are concerned about menstruation, and athletes are no exception. Thoughts and feelings about menstruation begin early and change throughout a woman's lifetime, but the concerns keep resurfacing. Young girls who haven't yet learned about the menstrual period lack these concerns. Once a girl has learned about it, though, she begins a subtle undercurrent of worry. Informed prepubertal girls wonder when they will get it, and menopausal women regret its loss, associating this loss with aging and the departure of some aspects of womanhood.

Athletic women, who are particularly attuned to bodily functions, are often more concerned than sedentary ones about whether their menstrual cycle is normal. Since menstruation is frequently associated with femininity, and since many women were taught to view exercise as "unfeminine" (an erroneous notion, of course), regular menstruation is especially reassuring to the physically active woman. Many athletic women are *inconvenienced* by menstrual bleeding, and some even claim that they would prefer not to menstruate. However, there is a big difference between not wanting to menstruate on the day of an important athletic event and never wanting to menstruate at all. Although some women deny their true feelings about this monthly event, most women would choose to be normal in every way and would like to have a monthly period as a visible sign that they are "normal" women.

WHAT IS NORMAL?

Between the ages of puberty and menopause, women are concerned about how much, how often, and how long they bleed. Of greatest importance is how often they bleed; how much and how long can vary a lot and still be normal. Your *menstrual interval* is the number of days from the beginning of one period to the beginning of your next period. If this interval is between 25 and 35 days, you have *regular* periods and are probably very normal from a reproductive point of view. If you menstruate more often than every 25 days or less often than every 35 days, you should consult your gynecologist to find out what is wrong. Either of these conditions is considered *irregular*. If you stop menstruating altogether, you have a condition called *amenorrhea*.

In a normal cycle, your ovaries make estrogen all the time, but different amounts of this hormone at different times of the cycle. The first part of the cycle, called the *follicular phase,* extends from the first day of menstruation until an egg is released at ovulation. Estrogen levels are very low in the early follicular phase and very high in the late follicular phase. Estrogen makes the inner lining of the uterus (the *endometrium*) grow. The second part of the cycle, called the *luteal phase,* extends from ovulation until the first day of your next menstrual period. During the luteal phase, the ovary that has just released an egg makes a lot of both estrogen and progesterone. Progesterone matures the endometrium once it has been stimulated by estrogen. At the end of the luteal phase, the concentrations of estrogen and progesterone fall, leading to shedding of the endometrium in the next menstrual period. (See Figure 6-1 showing phases of the menstrual cycle.)

Estrogen Deficiency

It is very important for you to have both estrogen and progesterone; a deficiency of either one can cause trouble. In addition to stimulating your endometrium, estrogen keeps your vagina moist and your bones thick and strong. Women who lack estrogen may develop dryness of the vagina, which can cause pain during intercourse. Since estrogen keeps calcium in your bones and helps you absorb more calcium from the foods you eat, women who have inadequate amounts of estrogen lose calcium from their bones and absorb less calcium from their foods. These tendencies lead to thinning of bones, osteoporosis, which is discussed in Chapter 1 and 9. Thin bones are more likely to break, and broken bones can lead to serious complications, including death. Thus, an estrogen deficiency is undesirable, and most women who stop menstruating for a long time (6 months or longer) have inadequate amounts of estrogen.

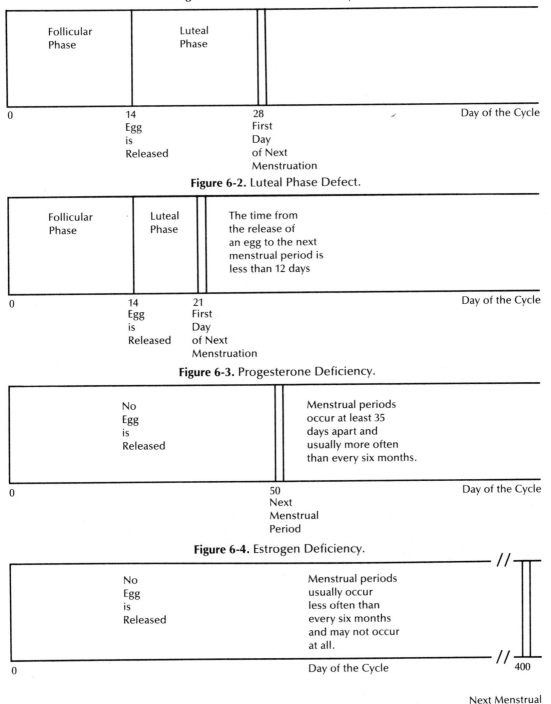

Figure 6-1. Normal Menstrual Cycle.

Follicular Phase | Luteal Phase

0 | 14 Egg is Released | 28 First Day of Next Menstruation | Day of the Cycle

Figure 6-2. Luteal Phase Defect.

Follicular Phase | Luteal Phase | The time from the release of an egg to the next menstrual period is less than 12 days

0 | 14 Egg is Released | 21 First Day of Next Menstruation | Day of the Cycle

Figure 6-3. Progesterone Deficiency.

No Egg is Released | Menstrual periods occur at least 35 days apart and usually more often than every six months.

0 | 50 Next Menstrual Period | Day of the Cycle

Figure 6-4. Estrogen Deficiency.

No Egg is Released | Menstrual periods usually occur less often than every six months and may not occur at all.

0 | Day of the Cycle | 400

Next Menstrual Period

Progesterone Deficiency

Most women who menstruate infrequently (between 35 and 100 days) do not ovulate. Such women have adequate amounts of estrogen but negligible amounts of progesterone. These women do not have to worry about their bones, but they should worry about overstimulation of the uterus. Since estrogen makes the endometrium grow and progesterone protects it from growing too much, women who have estrogen and lack progesterone are at risk of developing overstimulation of the endometrium, a condition that can progress to a cancer. Thus, a progesterone deficiency is dangerous for a woman who has normal amounts of estrogen. It is impossible to have normal amounts of progesterone with inadequate amounts of estrogen (except for a few extraordinarily rare diseases), so you don't have to worry about this possibility.

Can You Have a Hormone Deficiency Even if You Have Regular Periods?

Most, but not all, women who bleed every 25 to 35 days release an egg (ovulate) about 14 days before the beginning of the next period. A small percentage of women who have regular periods do not ovulate at all and thus shed the endometrium after only estrogen stimulation. These women are at risk of developing overstimulation of the endometrium, just as is true of many women with infrequent periods.

Luteal Phase Defect

Some women with regular periods ovulate, but don't make as much progesterone as they should afterward. This condition is called a *luteal phase defect* and is one of the first abnormalities that occur before a woman develops *athletic amenorrhea* or lack of menstruation associated with exercise. (Women who do not ovulate make virtually *no* progesterone, whereas women with luteal phase defects make *some* progesterone, but not enough.) A luteal phase defect imposes no proven risk of overstimulation or cancer, but it can make it harder for a woman to get pregnant. Since progesterone prepares the endometrium for the implantation of a fertilized egg, too little progesterone probably doesn't prepare the endometrium adequately for implantation.

Medication usually can correct this problem, enabling such fertile women to become mothers. (See Figures 6-2, 6-3, and 6-4, which demonstrate menstrual cycles in women with a luteal phase defect, progesterone deficiency, and estrogen deficiency.)

Can You Tell If and When You Ovulate?

It is easy to tell if and when you ovulate by taking your *basal body temperature* (BBT). Take your temperature with the same thermometer in the same site (mouth or rectum, but not switching) every morning before getting out of bed or moving around. Progesterone raises your basal body temperature, so it will be higher after ovulation, when your progesterone level is high. If you have regular menstrual periods and a normal luteal phase, your temperature will be low for the first 14 days or so of your cycle and then will rise and remain elevated for the next 12 to 14 days. (See Figure 6-5.) If your temperature remains elevated for 11 days or less, you probably have a luteal phase defect. If your temperature remains at the same level from one period to the next, you probably did not ovulate in that cycle, and there's a good chance that you don't ovulate at all. A luteal phase defect requires treatment only if you are trying to become pregnant and are having trouble doing so. If you don't ovulate, you *should* be treated, in order to prevent overstimulation of your uterus.

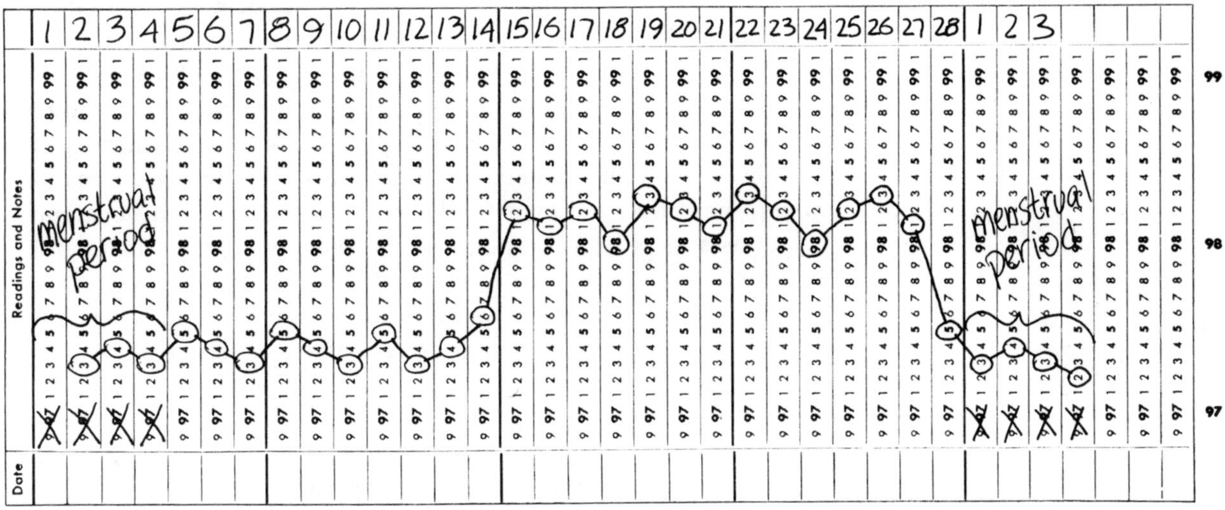

Figure 6-5. Basal Body Temperature Chart.

CAUSES OF IRREGULAR PERIODS AND AMENORRHEA

Before being treated for any menstrual problem, you should find out why you have the problem. Certain causes of these problems are serious and need attention. For example, irregular periods or amenorrhea can be caused by a tumor in your pituitary gland, producing too much of a hormone called prolactin. (Prolactin helps the breasts make milk after a woman gives birth; it also helps your body maintain normal menstrual cycles, but the mechanisms by which this happens aren't completely understood yet.) Such a tumor may grow and can cause blindness and even death.

An underactive thyroid gland can lead to these menstrual problems too, as well as to constipation, weight gain, fatigue, and lethargy. High levels of androgens (masculinizing hormones) can disrupt regular menstrual cyclicity and can also cause acne, facial hair growth, and male-pattern baldness. Menopause can also cause menstrual irregularity and amenorrhea, and this can occur earlier in life than expected. An early menopause in itself won't endanger your life, but you'd certainly want to know if this had happened.

EXERCISE AND MENSTRUAL IRREGULARITY OR AMENORRHEA

Irregular periods and amenorrhea are more common among athletic women than among the general population, but doctors don't know why. Many factors change when you exercise strenuously, any of which may contribute to the problem. You often lose both weight and fat when you train regularly, and weight loss or thinness may lead to menstrual disruption, even if you don't exercise. (See discussion of anorexia nervosa and bulimia in Chapter 8.) The physical stress of training may affect the menstrual cycle, possibly through hormone alterations and possibly through mechanisms we don't understand yet.

The emotional aspects of training and competition may also contribute to the problem. Although exercise tends to relieve stress and anxiety, it can also promote them. The psychological stress caused by competition is obvious. Less obvious, but equally important, is the emotional stress experienced by many recreational athletes. A working woman who is determined to incorporate a certain amount of exercise into her daily routine may experience considerable stress and anxiety in merely trying to coordinate all of her activities. These psychological factors may be more important than we realize and may contribute substantially to menstrual dysfunction. Any psychological stress can disrupt the delicate balance of carefully timed hormonal events necessary for regular ovulation and menstruation, and the stress associated with training and exercise can probably do this too.

Hormonal and Menstrual Changes with Exercise

Exercise causes temporary alterations in several hormones, including estrogen, progesterone, testosterone, prolactin, adrenaline, and noradrenaline. Most of these changes return to normal within an hour or two after cessation of exercise. Doctors don't know what effects, if any, result from these repeated transitory hormone changes. Women who exercise strenuously on a regular basis may develop some long-lasting hormone alterations, with the incidence rising as exercise is more strenuous, more prolonged, and more frequent. For example, women are more likely to develop a luteal phase defect when they increase their weekly running mileage. This minor disturbance may progress to a more serious condition: first, lack of ovulation with infrequent periods (in which the woman is still making estrogen but is not making progesterone), and then amenorrhea (with neither estrogen, progesterone, testosterone, prolactin, adrenaline, and noradrenaline. Most of these changes return to normal within an hour or independent of cause: (1) luteal phase defect, (2) infrequent periods without ovulation (progesterone deficiency), (3) total cessation of periods (estrogen deficiency). (See Figures 6-2, 6-3, and 6-4.)

WHAT TO DO IF YOU DON'T HAVE REGULAR PERIODS

As we discussed earlier, any woman who has irregular periods or amenorrhea should consult her gynecologist to find out if there is any serious cause for the problem (such as a pituitary gland tumor, an underactive thyroid gland, high androgen levels, or a premature menopause). If you have any of these problems, you will probably need further tests and will certainly need treatment.

Treatment for a Progesterone Deficiency

Even if no serious cause is found, you will probably need treatment in order to prevent a serious result. If you are making estrogen but not progesterone, you have an increased likelihood of developing cancer of the endometrium. Even before this happens, though, your periods will probably be heavy and infrequent, and they will probably occur at unpredictable, inconvenient times. If you have this condition, you should take progesterone pills for 10 consecutive days of every month. We recommend medroxyprogesterone acetate—10 milligrams daily on the first 10 days of every calendar month. If you have any unpleasant side effects while taking this, such as bloating, depression, increased appetite, or weight gain—any of which are usually mild when they occur and probably noticeably affect less than 5 percent of all women taking this drug—you may instead take only 5 milligrams daily on the first 10 days of every calendar month. You will probably begin a period within the first few days after taking the last pill. Don't worry if bleeding begins before you have finished all 10 pills. Take all 10 pills as scheduled anyway. This will prevent heavy bleeding episodes and will also prevent endometrial overstimulation and cancer.

Treatment for an Estrogen Deficiency

If you aren't making estrogen or progesterone, you have an increased likelihood of developing osteoporosis and vaginal dryness. Vaginal dryness can be treated when it develops, but osteoporosis should be prevented *before* it develops. You can't tell that your bones are getting thinner and more fragile unless you have their thickness and density measured with special machines (somewhat similar to X-rays).The first indication of bone thinning for most people is a fracture, and this usually means that serious and dangerous thinning has already occurred. If you have low levels of estrogen, you should take estrogen pills for 25 days of every month and progesterone pills as well on the last 10 days of the estrogen pills. Taking only estrogen would increase your chances of developing endometrial cancer and possibly breast cancer. We recommend conjugated estrogens—.625 or .9 milligrams daily on the first 25 days of every calendar month and medroxyprogesterone acetate—10 milligrams daily on days 16 through 25 of every calendar month. If you have any unpleasant side effects while taking the progesterone, you may instead take only 5 milligrams daily on days 16 through 25 of every month.

Birth Control Pills

Neither of these medication schedules (progesterone alone or estrogen and progesterone together) provides contraception. Your problem may resolve unexpectedly, and you may not realize this has happened. In fact, you can ovulate before having a spontaneous menstrual period. So if you are sexually active and don't want a pregnancy now, you should be using contraception. Birth control pills are a fine choice for women who have either an estrogen deficiency or a progesterone deficiency. Otherwise, you'll need medication *and* a reliable contraceptive method too. (See Chapter 10, where contraception is discussed in more detail.)

Who Should Not Take Estrogen?

Of the women who need estrogen either for contraception or for replacement of deficiencies, most can safely take estrogen without any problems, as long as they take progesterone too. However, certain women should *never* take estrogen, and others must decide whether the potential risks to them are worth it. Women who have active liver disease (such as hepatitis), women who have ever had an abnormal blood clot (such as a stroke, a heart attack, a pulmonary embolus, or thrombophlebitis), and women who have had endometrial cancer or breast cancer should never take estrogen. A *stroke* is caused by a clot in a blood vessel in your brain; a *heart attack* is caused by a clot in a blood vessel in your heart; a *pulmonary embolus* is a blood clot in your lung; and *thrombophlebitis* is any irritated vein with a blood clot in it, but often occurring in an arm or leg. Women who have migraine headaches, gall bladder disease, fibroid tumors (benign smooth-muscle tumors) of the uterus, diabetes, or high blood fat levels may experience more problems and risks if they take estrogen, and they should decide (in consultation with their doctor) whether the benefits of estrogen therapy outweigh these risks.

OTHER MENSTRUAL PROBLEMS

Though the most common menstrual problems that affect athletes are irregular periods and amenorrhea, many other menstrual disturbances may also occur. These include heavy bleeding at regular intervals and bleeding between periods.

Light Periods

Many women who have light periods wonder if this is cause for concern. It isn't. Although the usual duration of a menstrual period (the number of days you bleed and spot) is between three and five days, it is perfectly fine and even more convenient if you bleed less than three days. It is also fine to have such a light flow that you use very few tampons or sanitary napkins. Few women are this fortunate.

Prolonged or Heavy Periods

If your periods last longer than five days or if you bleed heavily and must change tampons or napkins often, you should check with your gynecologist to see if something is wrong. Heavy or prolonged periods can be caused by *fibroid tumors* (lumps of muscle) located inside the uterus, outside the uterus, or within the muscular wall of the uterus. Your gynecologist can usually tell if you have fibroids by examining you.

If you have fibroids, and if they are causing heavy bleeding or pain or are large or enlarging, you may want to have them removed. You can have just the tumors removed, or you can have your entire uterus removed *(hysterectomy)*. A hysterectomy is usually preferred if the woman has completed her family; a *myomectomy* (removal of just the fibroids) is usually done if she has not completed her family.

Another cause of heavy or prolonged periods is lack of progesterone. If you are producing estrogen but aren't ovulating and thus aren't producing progesterone, you are making your endometrium grow without limitation. This often leads to heavy or prolonged periods. While this hormone imbalance usually causes infrequent, irregular periods, menstruation with this condition may occur at regular, normal intervals too. As we discussed earlier, women who have this condition should take progesterone pills for 10 consecutive days every month. This treatment will lighten and shorten your periods if you have this condition.

Bleeding between Periods

Bleeding between periods *(intermenstrual bleeding)* is always abnormal. It may be caused by *polyps* (bunched-up pieces of the endometrium), by an irritation or tear of the cervix, or even by a cancer of the endometrium or cervix. If you have bright red bleeding between your periods, you should consult your gynecologist. Any visible sores on your cervix should be examined through a magnifying lens (in a procedure called a *biopsy*). If your cervix has no visible sores or other obvious bleeding sites, you need a *D&C*. This stands for *dilatation and curettage,* which means opening your cervix and scraping out your endometrium for microscopic examination.

If you have pink or brown spotting between your periods, particularly if accompanied by an odor, you may have a discharge from vaginitis. This should be checked by your gynecologist and can easily be treated. (See Chapter 10.)

SHOULD YOU STOP EXERCISING?

No, certainly not. Exercise isn't necessarily the culprit, even though some menstrual problems can be related to exercise or factors that are affected by regular exercise (such as weight, fat, or stress). Besides, the benefits you are receiving from your exercise are outweighing any possible negative factors. You should certainly continue to exercise, regardless of whether you have any of these problems. You should not stop exercising while you are being evaluated or treated. If you are very thin, though, you may want to consider gaining a few pounds, and if you suspect that you may be exercising too much (too vigorously, too often, or too long), you may want to try cutting back a bit. However, if you feel good at your present weight and exercise level, there is no reason to make any changes. What is important is that you feel good and comfortable about what you are doing.

MANIPULATING YOUR PERIODS WITH HORMONES

Menstrual periods that are frequent, prolonged, heavy, or unexpected may inconvenience you while you are training or competing. Although you can manipulate your periods by taking hormones, this practice is best reserved for elite athletes preparing for rare events of great importance. Frequent manipulation tends to cause more problems than it relieves. If you are a world-class athlete and are expecting to menstruate on the day of an extraordinarily important event, ask your gynecologist if you should take progesterone pills about two weeks before the event, to bring on your period early. Taking pills to delay your period until after the event may give you the same heavy, bloated feeling many women experience just before their periods begin (*premenstrual syndrome,* discussed below).

MENSTRUAL CRAMPS

It's perfectly safe, and even desirable, to exercise at all times of the month. Don't let menstrual or premenstrual discomfort interfere with your exercise routine.

Menstrual cramps are strong, intermittent lower abdominal pains that normally occur as often as once every minute on the first day or two of your menstrual period. They are usually a sign that you ovulated in the cycle just completed and, thus, that the reproductive parts of your body are functioning appropriately. These cramps are caused by chemicals called *prostaglandins,* which are produced by your endometrium and which cause your myometrium (the muscle of your uterus) to contract. During these contractions your uterus doesn't get enough blood and oxygen, and this deprivation is painful. Reassurance that menstrual cramps are normal may be somewhat comforting, but not comforting enough to compensate for the pain.

Many women experience less menstrual pain during exercise, and some notice less after they've been exercising on a regular basis. Don't expect to get total relief from this pain by exercising, though. Several drugs, called *prostaglandin inhibitors,* can prevent the formation of these pain-producing chemicals, as a result of which menstrual cramps can be totally prevented or relieved. Ask your gynecologist to prescribe one for you if you suffer from this discomfort. Examples of these drugs are ibuprofen (Brand name: Motrin), naproxen (Brand name: Naprosyn), naproxen sodium (Brand name: Anaprox), and mefenamic acid (Brand name: Ponstel).

A side benefit of these drugs is a reduction in menstrual blood flow, which is advantageous to exercising women for several reasons. First of all, less bleeding is more convenient. (It's hard to run your best marathon when you have to stop to change tampons several times along the course.) Second, less blood loss means less iron loss, so less likelihood of iron deficiency, which can impair your athletic performance.

Menstrual cramps are often accompanied by gastro-intestinal discomfort, such as nausea, vomiting, and diarrhea. These annoying problems are probably caused by prostaglandins too, and prostaglandin inhibitors will prevent them.

Normal menstrual cramps being within 24 hours of the start of menstrual bleeding (either before or after). If your menstrual cramps begin more than 24 hours before bleeding begins, or last more than two days after bleeding begins, they may be caused by an abnormal condition, such as endometriosis or a pelvic infection. (See Chapter 10.) Consult your gynecologist if you think you have one of these disorders.

PREMENSTRUAL SYNDROME

Premenstrual syndrome (PMS) is a group of symptoms that women experience during the few days before menstruation begins. Although these symptoms are probably caused by normal hormones produced at that time of the menstrual cycle or by some by-products of these hormones, doctors still do not know which hormones are responsible and how they produce the undesirable effects. The symptoms of this disorder fall into four major categories: (1) anxiety (including jitteriness and insomnia), (2) depression (including mood swings), (3) increased appetite (including specific food cravings), and (4) fluid retention (including headaches, breast soreness, hand swelling, feet swelling, leg heaviness during exercise, and weight gain). While the first two categories are emotional and the last two physical, all four are caused by chemical changes or imbalances. (The chemicals for each category haven't been identified yet, though.)

Many women exeeperience fewer and milder symptoms when they exercise. But 50 to 75 percent of all women have some or all of these symptoms at least some of the time, and exercise rarely eliminates them completely. Don't despair if you have these symptoms. Chart your symptoms on your basal body temperature (BBT) chart, so that you can see whether you are ovulating and whether the symptoms come only before your period. Many women who think their symptoms occur premenstrually are surprised to find, when they actually record them, that they occur randomly throughout the menstrual cycle. Bring your BBT chart to your gynecologist, and discuss your symptoms while looking at your BBT chart. If you truly have PMS, your doctor may prescribe medication to help you. At the present time, the drug spironolactone appears to be more effective than most other drugs, although more studies are needed to find the best drug for this problem. This drug is extremely safe and is widely used for several conditions, such as high blood pressure and excessive body hair. Side effects are very rare.

If your symptoms occur not only before your period, but also at other times, you probably have another problem, not PMS. In that case, you may need other medication. If you experience anxiety, depression, or mood swings (rather than breast soreness, swelling, or increased appetite) that are not solely premenstrual, you may need to consult a psychiatrist, who is the best trained specialist to evaluate your problem and prescribe any necessary medication. Many people are offended by the suggestion to see a psychologist or psychotherapist, when they should actually be flattered. Talking out a problem usually doesn't help people who have limited intelligence. It is intelligent people who are most likely to be helped by gaining the insight that a psychotherapist can help them acquire. All people have problems, and most people would be helped by discussing their problems with a specialist. However, few are willing enough to invest the time and money necessary for psychotherapy. While a psychologist, a psychotherapist, and a psychiatrist can all furnish great insight, only a psychiatrist can prescribe medication. This may offer an advantage to consulting a psychiatrist directly.

If you experience breast soreness, swelling, or bloating that is not solely premenstrual, you should consult an internist.

SUMMARY

In summary, menstruation and its accompanying discomfort are normal feminine events. Don't let them interfere with your exercise program. If menstruation presents any problems for you, consult your gynecologist to find out whether anything is wrong and whether you need treatment. But keep exercising!

7 PREGNANCY AND AFTERWARD

Pregnancy should be considered extra training and you should prepare for this added effort just as you would prepare for any athletic event. You should become fit before you become pregnant and should plan to maintain this fitness throughout pregnancy. The key to exercise during pregnancy is prepregnancy fitness. You certainly won't want to stop exercising for nine months after you've worked so hard to become lean and strong. If you *do* stop, you'll lose much of the fitness you gained before.

Physical fitness is certainly good for the mother, but doctors haven't yet determined how much exercise a mother-to-be can safely do to attain and maintain physical fitness without endangering the baby she's carrying. Until this question is resolved, certain precautions are necessary.

CONCERNS ABOUT EXERCISE DURING PREGNANCY

Blood Flow

Mother and baby have separate blood systems, and mixing of these two bloods does not take place except in very rare circumstances. However, nutrients are filtered from the mother's blood to the baby's. Hence, adequate nutrition for the baby depends upon an adequately nourished blood supply from the mother. Blood flow to the mother's uterus is important because this filtering from mother's blood to baby's takes place in the mother's uterus.

During exercise, less blood flows to certain organs, such as your liver and kidneys, while more flows to your skin and your exercising muscles. At a certain level of exertion, blood will be diverted away from your uterus where your baby is resting and growing. Doctors don't know at what level of exertion there will be a decline in the blood supply to your uterus, nor how much of a decline in its blood supply a fetus can safely withstand. It is probably reasonable to continue exercising at the same level of exertion you were accustomed to before pregnancy, but it *may* not be safe to exercise more vigorously or more frequently than that. Since a pregnant woman does more work even at rest, compared to her nonpregnant state, and since she is also carrying more weight than she did before pregnancy, she should be prepared to slow down. This means that a woman who was accustomed to running six-minute miles before pregnancy will probably have to settle for eight- or nine-minute miles during pregnancy. You can usually tell how hard you are working by how hard and fast you have to breathe, and you should exercise at the level that *seems* like your prepregnancy level, based on your breathing and overall effort. As you approach the end of your pregnancy, you'll be carrying a lot more weight and will be working much harder at any given pace, compared to your prepregnancy effort at that pace. Expect to slow down considerably by the end of your pregnancy.

Excessive Heat

Exercise raises your body temperature and can raise it dangerously high. The *hyperthermia* (high temperature) experienced by some marathon runners isn't dangerous in the nonpregnant state, but it can be dangerous in the pregnant state. Hyperthermia in early pregnancy (during the first two months) can lead to birth defects, particularly those involving the development of the brain and spinal cord. In later pregnancy (after the fourth month), hyperthermia can lead to premature labor. Doctors don't know of any specific proven dangers from hyperthermia during the third and fourth months, but it's probably best to avoid hyperthermia at this stage of pregnancy too.

You should check your temperature immediately at the end of your customary exercise session (preferably by armpit or rectum, which are more accurate sites than the mouth). If your temperature exceeds 101 degrees Fahrenheit, you should take steps to keep cooler. Such measures may include exercising at a cooler time of day and for a shorter period of time, wearing lighter or looser clothing, and drinking more fluids. (Dehydration enhances the temperature rise that occurs during exercise.) Since body temperature can climb in a sauna, whirlpool, hot tub, or steam room, you should either avoid visiting these places during pregnancy or limit your exposures to 10 minutes or less. Check your temperature at the end of visits to such hot environments to be safe.

Low Oxygen Supply

Since a developing baby requires adequate oxygen, any activities or environments that may reduce the fetus's oxygen supply should probably be avoided during pregnancy. For example, sprinting or training at high altitudes may reduce the oxygen going to the baby. Since we don't know how much of a reduction, if any, can be tolerated safely, it is better to choose activities that pose no risk.

Deep-sea diving subjects your body and that of your baby to increased pressure. Pressures deeper than those at 30 to 60 feet may be dangerous, although we don't know this for sure. If you *must* dive during pregnancy, it's probably a good idea to limit your ventures to shallower depths. Nitrogen levels in the bloodstream change as divers go up and down. Such changes can lead to illness (decompression sickness) even in the nonpregnant state. Until we know more about the limits of safety during dives, sports that involve deep dives should probably be avoided.

Abdominal Trauma

Anything that strikes a pregnant woman's abdomen endangers the baby inside. The baby itself is actually cushioned very well. In early pregnancy, the fetus is well protected by the bones and muscles of the mother's pelvis; in later pregnancy, the baby is well protected by the ample cushion of amniotic fluid. However, a sudden blow to the abdomen may cause premature separation of the placenta (the afterbirth), an event that could kill the baby. Thus, sports like boxing, fencing, and springboard diving should be avoided. Sports involving balance impose some risks during pregnancy because of the pregnant woman's unaccustomedness to her altered center of gravity. Thus, sports like downhill skiing are safe only if a pregnant woman can avoid falling on her abdomen.

Animal Studies

Several animal studies have shown some worrisome results. Animals that exercised strenuously, repetitively, and for a long time often gave birth to baby animals that had stunted fetal growth or who died shortly before or after birth. Sometimes the exercising mother animals entered labor prematurely too. In some cases, prepregnancy exercise was somewhat protective, but not always. There are certainly differences among the various animals that have been studied. Certain animals can exercise strenuously without obvious untoward effect on their fetuses, while others show fetal harm with very little exercise. We don't really know whether we can draw conclusions about humans based on any of the animals that have been studied. We also do not know whether the harmful effects in animals are due to inadequate blood flow, high temperature, or some other factor. Nevertheless, these animal studies are alarming and give us cause for concern about exercising humans.

GUIDELINES FOR EXERCISING DURING PREGNANCY

Despite the potential dangers to the fetus that have already been discussed (including inadequate blood flow, high temperatures, abdominal trauma, low oxygen availability, and harmful effects shown in animals), physical fitness remains desirable for the pregnant woman. Pregnancy, labor, and delivery are hard work, and hard work is easier and safer for both mother and baby if the mother is physically fit. Besides, most regular exercisers won't want to stop for nine months, and there is no conclusive evidence at the present time that they *should* stop exercising altogether.

If you have a normal pregnancy and if you were accustomed to aerobic exercise before you became pregnant, you can probably continue exercising throughout pregnancy as long as you have no problems or complications. Check with your obstetrician first, of course, to be sure everything is normal. If so, you can probably continue exercising at the same level of *perceived* exertion right until the day you deliver. Despite some old wives' tales to the contrary, exercising does not increase a woman's chances of having a miscarriage or stillbirth. Such misfortunes usually raise many feelings of guilt in women who experience them, and it is common for a woman

Warnings

1. Exercise during pregnancy only if your pregnancy is normal and without complications.
2. Check with your obstetrician before exercising during pregnancy, to be sure that it's okay to do so.

Danger Signs

1. Pain
2. Bleeding
3. Rupture of membranes (breaking bag of water)
4. No kicking or fetal movement

Remember

1. Listen to your body.
2. Avoid fatigue and excessive heat.
3. Stop exercising and see your obstetrician immediately if any problems arise.

to wonder whether she did anything to contribute to her accident. Most miscarriages are caused by abnormalities in the fetus's chromosomes, which are unaffected by anything you do. There is no evidence that exercise has any effect at all on a woman's chance of having a miscarriage or stillbirth, and it is unfortunate that feelings of guilt accompany such experiences so often.

Pain, bleeding, rupture of membranes (breaking your bag of water), and absence of fetal movement (not feeling the baby move) are danger signals in any pregnancy. If you have any of these problems, stop exercising immediately and let your obstetrician know about the symptoms. Don't resume exercising until your obstetrician has determined that you can do so safely.

If you weren't accustomed to aerobic exercise before pregnancy, you should not engage in any endurance sport more strenuous than walking during pregnancy.

Stretching and strengthening exercises are fine for all pregnant women, even if they never engaged in these activities before. So calisthenics and weight-training are recommended for all women who have normal, uncomplicated pregnancies.

Dangerous Sports

Any sport that leads to a potential low oxygen supply or hyperthemia for the fetus, or abdominal trauma to the mother represents a danger to the fetus. Endurance sports such as running, bicycling, cross-

SPORTS RECOMMENDED THROUGHOUT PREGNANCY

Walking	Swimming
Jogging	Volleyball
Hiking	Golf
Aerobic dancing	Bowling
Other fast dancing	Frisbee
Gymnastics	Sailing
Calisthenics	Waterskiing
Bicycling	Downhill skiing
Baseball	Cross-country skiing
Softball	Rowing
Basketball	Canoeing
Touch football	Ice skating
Racquetball	Roller skating
Squash	Archery
Paddleball	Yoga
Handball	Javelin
Tennis	Discus
Badminton	Table tennis

SPORTS TO AVOID THROUGHOUT PREGNANCY

Hang gliding*	Hockey
Sky diving*	Soccer
Deep-sea diving	Tackle football
Springboard diving	Competitive track and field
Parachute-jumping*	(except for javelin and
Boxing*	discus)
Fencing	

(All of the above are discouraged because they impose potential dangers to the fetus. The sports marked by * also impose dangers to the mother.)

country skiing, aerobic dancing, and swimming may reduce the fetus's oxygen supply or raise the fetus's temperature, particularly if continued longer than 30 minutes in each session; women unaccustomed to these sports should not begin them during pregnancy. In addition to the sports already mentioned, hang gliding, parachute jumping, sky diving, and tackle football impose a risk of abdominal trauma, and such sports should be avoided. Hockey and soccer present risks of both inadequate blood and oxygen and potential abdominal trauma and should be avoided too. Competitive track and any other speed work should be avoided because they may reduce the fetus's blood supply.

We feel that hang gliding, sky diving, parachute-jumping, and boxing are dangerous for everyone, including nonpregnant women and men.

Nutrition

A sedentary pregnant woman requires more calories than she did in the non-pregnant state, and an exercising woman needs more calories than a sedentary one. Exercising pregnant women must be sure to get enough calories to provide energy for themselves, their pregnancies, and their exercise. Not all pregnant athletes do this.

During pregnancy, your daily diet should contain about 80 grams of protein, at least 1,500 milligrams of calcium, about one milligram of folic acid, and about 80 milligrams of iron. These requirements are the same whether you are exercising or not. However, your total caloric needs will be greater if you are exercising. How many calories you need depends on how much you weigh and how active you are.

The best way to judge how much you should eat is by your appetite and your scale. Your appetite is generally a good guide, particularly if you are getting a consistent amount of exercise. In that case, your scale will reflect weight gain from pregnancy. As you know, changes in exercise quantity can also produce changes in weight, due to gains in muscles and losses of fat with exercise and the opposite effects with cessation of exercise. So if you get more or less exercise than you were accustomed to before you became pregnant, your weight may change due to changes in body composition that are unrelated to pregnancy. Such alterations will, of course, confuse the picture of how adequately you are eating. As we mentioned earlier, we do not recommend getting *more* exercise during pregnancy than you did before you were pregnant.

A pregnant woman should gain approximately 20 to 30 pounds by the time she is ready to give birth. Woman who gain less than 20 pounds during their pregnancy are more likely to give birth to small babies. Small birth weight increases a baby's chances of suffering from many health problems. Women who gain more than 30 pounds are probably gaining too much fat, which may be hard to lose afterward. Although the average weight gain by the end of the third month is 2 to 4 pounds, many pregnant women actually lose a few pounds during early pregnancy because of morning sickness and consequent difficulty keeping food down. Average weight gain should be nearly one pound per week after the first three months have passed.

Throughout your pregnancy, your obstetrician will be measuring the size and growth of your uterus too. Depending on whether your weight gain and uterine growth are adequate, you may need to undergo additional tests of your baby's growth and maturity, such as a *sonogram*. This particular test is like an X-ray study, but it uses safe sound waves rather than dangerous radiation. Your obstetrician will tell you if a sonogram is indicated.

BREAST-FEEDING

As we mentioned earlier, you'll need to consume enough fluids if you're exercising during pregnancy, in order to avoid dehydration and the hyperthermia that may follow. Breast-feeding athletes require the same amounts of all nutrients as they needed throughout pregnancy. You'll need the same number of calories and the same amounts of proteins, vitamins, and minerals. In addition, you'll need enough fluids to replace what you're losing in both perspiration and milk.

HOW SOON CAN YOU RESUME EXERCISING AFTER DELIVERY?

Listen to your body, which will tell you when to resume exercising after delivery. If you had a normal vaginal delivery, you can probably resume exercising as soon as you can do so without pain. An *episiotomy* is a surgical cut on your perineum (the outer tissue between the openings of your vagina and rectum), with stitches to repair this incision. Such a cut is usually performed to prevent the tissues from tearing or overstretching as the baby's head emerges. It also reduces the trauma the baby's head experiences in coming out. An episiotomy usually causes soreness to last longer than without such a cut, and this may make bicycling or running particularly uncomfortable during the first few days after delivery. Since pain is an indication that healing is incomplete, you can probably do just about anything as soon as you want to, as long as the activity doesn't hurt. The only exceptions to this are swimming and other water sports, which may lead to bacterial infection of your female organs. When you give birth, your cervix (the mouth of your uterus) is wide open, and it takes a few weeks to close. Until it has closed, bacteria and other infecting organisms can enter your uterus, which normally is sterile (germ-free). Thus, nothing should enter your vagina until your cervix has closed, including a penis, tampon, douche, or water. So avoid the entry of any of these for at least three weeks after giving birth.

If you have had a Cesarean section delivery (birth of your baby through an incision in your abdomen), your abdominal and overall soreness will be greater than after a vaginal delivery. This will make it more painful to exercise soon after giving birth. You should postpone exercising after a Cesarean section too until you can do so without pain.

SUMMARY

Get in shape before you become pregnant. Pregnancy, labor, and delivery are hard work, and you'll be better able to do this work if you're physically fit. As long as your pregnancy is normal and your obstetrician agrees with the plan, you can probably maintain your fitness throughout pregnancy and afterward.

8 YOUNG GIRLS

Young girls should develop the regular exercise habit at an early age, and they should continue to practice that habit throughout life. When you were a school girl, you were probably given the misleading message that exercise was "unladylike" and so were the perspiration and odors that often accompany it. This bad advice created several generations of fat, sedentary women with a lot of medical problems as a result.

MOTIVATING YOUNG GIRLS TO EXERCISE

Exercise *is* good for little girls, from infancy on. They are as well suited to vigorous exercise as little boys, and exercise will become even more essential for girls than for boys as they pass into their mature years when women become more susceptible than men to osteoporosis and obesity. (See Chapter 9.) Young girls should learn to exercise because it's fun, not because it pleases their parents or because they win medals. Many young competitive athletes stop exercising altogether after a few tough years. Sometimes they regret having missed childhood fun while they were training and competing. They may also be rebelling against the parents and coaches they were pleasing with their successes. Those who compete without success often drop out too, since it isn't much fun to lose all the time. These "athletic failures" become sedentary adults, and they often have difficulty accepting any worthwhile exercise as fun after so many years of psychological pain.

Schools have changed greatly in their attitudes toward girl athletes. Being a "tomboy" had a negative connotation in the past, but a more accurate picture now is that of an agile, energetic, and coordinated girl. How fortunate to be born with such assets and to be encouraged to cultivate them!

The same rules of training used for adults apply to children too. (See Chapter 1.) Young girls can strengthen their heart muscles as well as their arms and legs. Children follow the same formula as adults to calculate the target heart rate at which they must exercise in order to strengthen the heart muscle. Since children are much younger, they have higher maximum heart rates than adults and usually higher target heart rates too. For example, 10-year-old Cindy has a maximum heart rate of 220 minus 10, which is 210. Her resting heart rate is

SPORTS RECOMMENDED FOR YOUNG GIRLS

Walking	Swimming
Jogging	Volleyball
Hiking	Table tennis
Aerobic dancing	Frisbee
Other fast dancing	Sailing
Gymnastics	Basketball
Calisthenics	Waterskiing
Bicycling	Downhill skiing
Baseball	Cross-country skiing
Softball	Rowing
Tackle football	Canoeing
Touch football	Ice skating
Racquetball	Roller skating
Squash	Archery
Paddleball	Yoga
Soccer	Springboard diving
Tennis	Competitive track and field
Badminton	

SPORTS YOUNG GIRLS SHOULD AVOID

Hang gliding	Fencing
Deep-sea diving	Hockey
Parachute-jumping	Bowling
Handball	Golf
Boxing	

70. So, her heart rate reserve is 210 minus 70, which is 140. Half of her heart rate reserve is 70. Her target heart rate, then, is 70 plus 70, which is 140. (Remember that the average adult target heart rate is about 120.) Like adults, children should exercise continuously at their target heart rate or higher for at least 10 minutes and should repeat this at least twice each week in order to strengthen the heart muscle.

STRENGTHENING THE SKELETAL MUSCLES

To strengthen any muscle a child must contract the muscle against resistance, as an adult must do. The same rules of weight training apply for children as for adults. However, young girls have lower levels of the masculinizing hormone testosterone than do adult women, and young girls don't have enough of this hormone to increase the size or strength of their muscles greatly. (As we have already discussed, testosterone helps to enlarge and strengthen muscles, while the feminizing hormone estrogen promotes fat formation. Adult women have much lower levels of testosterone than do adult men, and the average man is much stronger than the average woman as a result.) Before puberty, both girls and boys have low levels of testosterone. So neither girls nor boys can enlarge or strengthen their muscles greatly even by lifting weights.

POTENTIAL INJURIES

Lifting heavy weights can impose excessive force on the open growth plates of young bones, thereby damaging them. This can interfere with subsequent growth. Although such injuries occur rarely, the risks of weight training before puberty probably outweigh any potential gains in strength. Lighter weights will be safer but won't lead to greater strength. Recent reports from Bulgaria show that young children can lift very heavy weights without incurring injuries. Naim Suleimanov, a 16-year-old who is probably the greatest weight lifter ever, started lifting weights when he was nine.

Other sports can damage a child's growth plates too, though such injuries are even rarer than with weight training. Some doctors are concerned about possible damage to the growth plates during long-distance running in particular, even though running injuries to growth plates are extraordinarily uncommon. The growth plate (the epiphysis) is the center from which growth takes place in the long bones. As long as a growth plate remains open, its bone is capable of continued growth. An open growth plate remains weaker than the rest of the bone and is more susceptible to breaking when subjected to excessive force. Because an injury to a growth plate on a leg bone could lead to less ultimate growth in that bone, which could produce a shorter leg, some doctors advise children to avoid long-distance running. However, we feel this caution is unwarranted, based on the rarity of such injuries and the unlikelihood of such injuries to cause lasting harm when they do occur. Several studies have shown that stress fractures rarely occur at open growth plates and that in any case they rarely interfere with a child's ultimate bone growth. Stress fractures in the feet, legs, and pelvis are common running injuries in both adults and children. However, there is no evidence that children are more susceptible than adults to these fractures. Nor is there any evidence that stress fractures interfere with a child's ultimate growth.

Although doctors don't know all of the long-term effects of long-distance running in childhood, it seems pretty safe for children to run long distances, as long as it's their idea to do so (not their parents' idea).

FLEXIBILITY

The same rules of flexibility training apply to children and adults (described in Chapter 1), but children are naturally much more flexible than adults and have to do very little work to maintain this flexibility. Children have greater natural flexibility because their muscles, tendons, and ligaments haven't lost the elasticity that declines with aging. Flexibility is best achieved through slow, controlled motions that attempt to increase the range of motion of joints. By training to accommodate the specific movements involved in practicing any particular sport, children will be less likely to get injured.

CAN BOYS AND GIRLS COMPETE WITH EACH OTHER?

Since they have similar low levels of testosterone, boys and girls can compete with each other fairly until they reach puberty. After puberty boys produce much more testosterone, while girls produce only a bit more, and girls produce much more estrogen, while boys produce only a bit more. So after puberty the average boy gets taller and stronger than the average girl, who gets fatter, particularly if she doesn't exercise. So boys and girls can't compete with each other fairly *after* puberty.

BODY COMPOSITION CHANGES DURING PUBERTY

The changes in a girl's body as she goes through puberty may affect her suitability to participate and compete successfully in certain sports. As she makes more estrogen, she stops growing taller. Girls who enter puberty at a younger age tend to be shorter as adults because their bodies stopped growing sooner. When Joni entered puberty, she developed rounder contours as she added fat to surfaces that were flat before—for example, her breasts, her hips, and her thighs. This gave her a womanly shape. Since she must carry her fat with her in all athletic competition, she must do more work at any specified level of performance (e.g., running a seven-minute mile). As a result, these womanly changes impose an athletic disadvantage for most sports. (Sumo wrestling may be an exception!) So some former athletes may drop out when pubertal body changes make them less successful in certain types of competition. Joni dropped out for that very reason!

On the other hand, the added estrogen that puberty gives a girl promotes stronger, thicker bones, which add durability. In addition, puberty raises a girl's testosterone level a bit—not enough to masculinize her appearance, but enough to strengthen her bones with routine activities, and enough to strengthen her muscles with weight training.

Of course, in sports that require skill and coordination, much improvement comes with practice. As discussed in Chapter 1, sports like tennis require that you teach your brain to coordinate your muscles properly. Practice cultivates these skills, and puberty has no effect on them.

The physical changes in a girl's body during puberty are generally permanent—that is, she will not get significantly taller, and her tendency to form fat will remain. However, these estrogen-related changes may be lessened in some women who become very thin and have low estrogen levels with amenorrhea. These women certainly won't get any taller, but the thinness that may have contributed to their low estrogen levels may be perpetuated by the same low estrogen level. (See Chapter 6.)

SOCIAL CHANGES DURING PUBERTY

Physical changes are not the only alterations a young girl faces at puberty. Accompanying the development of her woman's curves, she becomes interested in boys and dating. Friendships with other girls often take on greater importance too. Puberty is a difficult time for all girls (obviously for all boys too), and most girls feel a tremendous need to be exactly like most of their friends—in size, shape, interests, fashion. Those who were athletes before puberty may lose interest in sports as social interests surpass all others. Some former athletes may be discouraged from continued exercise by peer pressure to conform socially.

That's exactly what happened to Denise, who became more interested in how her face and hair looked to the boys in her class than in the running she'd enjoyed before. Since running left her sweaty, and she didn't have enough time to fix her hair and apply new makeup between her shower and her evening club meetings, she stopped running altogether. (See Chapter 12 for advice about hair and cosmetics.)

HOW DO EXERCISE AND PUBERTY AFFECT EACH OTHER?

Athletic girls tend to experience their first menstrual period (called *menarche*, which is a late pubertal event) at a later age than their sedentary friends. (Menarche occurs at an average age of 12½ years in the United States; among athletic girls it occurs at an average age of 13½ to 15½.) The fact that exercise and delayed menarche are related doesn't mean that they have a cause-and-effect relationship with each other. Doctors don't know whether a cause-and-effect relationship exists, and if it does exist, which factor is cause and which is effect: Does exercise delay puberty, or does a delayed puberty help to make a women a better athlete? Probably both factors affect each other, making the picture even less clear.

Some scientists believe that a girl needs to have a certain amount of body fat or a certain body weight in order to begin to menstruate. If such a level exists, it probably differs among women. Menarche tends to occur at a later age in thin women, heavy exercisers, and those who have poor nutrition and serious illnesses. If thinness delays menarche (a hypothesis that hasn't been proven), exercise may help to delay menarche by promoting thinness.

On the other hand, if a girl loses much of her interest in sports because pubertal changes have made her fatter and less successful as an athlete, she may drop out as a result. In this case, a delay of puberty might be helping her friends to surpass her in athletic success. So it remains unclear whether exercise delays puberty or a delayed puberty promotes athletic success and perseverance.

IS A DELAYED MENARCHE HARMFUL?

As long as menarche has occurred by the age of 18, a delay is not medically harmful. A delay that lasts later than age 18 is usually accompanied by a low estrogen level that promotes thinning and weakening of bones. This *can* be dangerous. Even among those who begin menstruating by the age of 18, a delay can be psychologically harmful. The usual peer pressures and difficulties of adolescence make it emotionally traumatic for a teenage girl to be different from her friends. Girls who experience this psychological discomfort need special understanding and support. Fear of a potential pubertal delay should not discourage girls from exercising.

WHEN SHOULD A GIRL CONSULT A DOCTOR?

Any girl who has not begun to menstruate by the age of 16 should have a pelvic examination performed. Any girl who has not begun to develop breasts or underarm hair or pubic hair by the age of 14 should be examined also. What the doctor finds in this examination will determine whether tests are needed and treatment too. Two other conditions should always bring a young girl to a doctor: vaginal bleeding or discharge before the age of 9. None of these conditions should prevent a girl from exercising, though.

No girl is too young to have a pelvic examination, and a first pelvic examination for any girl or woman should always be accompanied by an explanation of what is being done, why it is being done, and how it will feel. No normal woman can or should be expected to cooperate and relax during her first pelvic examination without such an explanation.

OTHER GYNECOLOGIC PROBLEMS IN TEENAGERS

The same problems that affect older women who menstruate can affect teenagers too, including irregular periods, amenorrhea, and menstrual cramps. These should usually be evaluated and treated in the same thorough manner as for older women, even though serious causes are much less common among teenagers.

One exception to this rule involves the treatment of teenagers with irregular periods or amenorrhea. These conditions are much more common among adolescents than among older women. Because most teenagers suffer no harm from these conditions within the first year they exist, it is acceptable to postpone treatment for as long as a year. However, some girls may experience profuse bleeding episodes (probably because they are making estrogen but not progesterone) during the first year of this problem. So it is equally acceptable to begin treatment sooner, to avoid the possibility of such heavy bleeding episodes. Waiting longer than a year to begin treatment can lead to serious complications from an estrogen or progesterone deficiency. Teenagers who have an estrogen deficiency may develop bone thinning and a greater susceptibility to fractures. Those who have a progesterone deficiency are likely to have profuse bleeding episodes from time to time, and these can lead to anemia.

Except for the acceptability of waiting as long as a year to begin treatment, teenagers and adults should have the same evaluation and treatment for irregular periods and amenorrhea. (See Chapter 6.)

Teenagers who have uncomfortable menstrual cramps should be treated with the same prostaglandin inhibitors that are prescribed for adults, and in the same dosages. Minor cramps may be tolerated without treatment, but cramps that are strong enough to be at all distracting should be treated.

NUTRITION

Exercising girls require more calories than sedentary girls, but daily requirements for most nutrients do not increase with exercise. Exercise increases requirements only for niacin, thiamine, riboflavin, and pantothenic acid, but a child will get adequate amounts of these vitamins if she eats a balanced diet. Children require less of most nutrients than do adults, primarily because they are smaller.

In most cases, a child who eats to satisfy her hunger will consume enough calories to meet the needs of both exercise and normal growth. However, the common teenage obsession with thinness has led some girls to starve themselves in an effort to be slender. Some girls do this because they have a distorted body image of how they really look. Ballerinas often starve themselves because they will lose their jobs if they gain a few pounds. Until recently, many coaches encouraged their young athletes to starve themselves, in order to shed fat, since fat impedes athletic performance. Coaches have become much more aware of the prevalance of extreme dieting among athletes and of the hazards of this practice. Fewer coaches are encouraging extreme thinness now, but both ballerinas and athletes may be subjected to external pressure to become and remain thin, even though being too thin can be dangerous. If you know anyone who is dieting excessively by either self-imposed or outside standards, urge her to get professional help.

Anorexia nervosa is an eating disorder that is more common among women than among men. Its victims starve themselves and remain very active. They see themselves as fat, although they appear emaciated to the rest of the world. People can die from this disease! *Bulimia* is another eating disorder, also more common among women than among men. Those who have this disorder alternately starve and binge, and they can harm themselves in either phase (fasting or feasting).

Women with either of these eating disorders frequently stop menstruating. As we discussed in Chapter 6, amenorrhea is common among thin women and those who lose weight by any means. These two eating disorders are particularly serious and almost always need professional treatment.

SUMMARY

In summary, young girls should be encouraged to exercise regularly and to continue this habit as they get older. Weight training with heavy weights may be somewhat dangerous, and lighter weights will be ineffective in adding strength. Aerobic and flexibility training are desirable for all young girls.

Any young girl who experiences delayed puberty, irregular periods, amenorrhea, or menstrual cramps should be evaluated and treated for her problem, and she *should* continue exercising.

9 OLDER WOMEN

WHAT IS THE MENOPAUSE?

The menopause occurs when your ovaries run out of functioning eggs, and it is marked by your final menstrual period. Some eggs actually remain in your ovaries, but eggs do not respond well to the normal signals they receive from your pituitary gland. The normal hormones made in your pituitary gland which stimulate your ovaries are called follicle stimulating hormone (FSH) and luteinizing hormone (LH). In women of reproductive age, FSH and LH lead the ovaries to make estrogen and progesterone, as well as to mature and release an egg each month. When the only eggs remaining in your ovaries are incapable of responding to FSH and LH, the pituitary gland makes a tremendous amount of FSH and LH, in an attempt to "beat a dead horse." So women who have passed the menopause have high blood levels of FSH and LH. After the menopause, your ovaries will make much less estrogen, and this can cause problems, such as osteoporosis and vaginal dryness.

Fat women are much less likely to develop an estrogen deficiency after the menopause because their fat tissue makes estrogen, unrelated to whether the ovaries are making any or not. This estrogen production from fat helps to protect an obese woman from developing osteoporosis, but it increases her risk of developing endometrial cancer (cancer of the inner lining of the uterus).

IS EXERCISE DANGEROUS FOR OLDER WOMEN?

Older women need regular exercise most, and unfortunately many were socially and culturally programmed to be sedentary. Although many women over the age of 50 believe that exercise is dangerous for them, it is actually dangerous for them *not* to exercise.

WHAT CAN EXERCISE DO?

Several problems are common among women after the reproductive years have passed. These include osteoporosis, heart disease, hot flushes, vaginal dryness, obesity and depression. Some of these problems are due to a lack of estrogen, and these usually can be corrected with estrogen therapy. Exercise can help to prevent or relieve some of these too.

OSTEOPOROSIS

Osteoporosis is the most serious problem among older women. Twenty-five percent of all Caucasian women over the age of 60 will break a bone from this disease, and some of them may die from complications of such an accident. In men the process of bone thinning begins around the age of 50, but in women this process begins around the age of 20. Since men have thicker and stronger bones than women before the bone loss begins, and since bone loss occurs at a slower pace in men than in women, older women tend to have much thinner bones and many more fractures than older men. The factors that increase a woman's chances of developing osteoporosis are being thin, being Caucasian or Oriental, being sedentary, smoking cigarettes, drinking excessive alcohol, eating inadequate dietary calcium, living to an old age, and having parents with osteoporosis. Although fat women are much less likely to develop osteoporosis, we don't recommend obesity for prevention, since it imposes a lot of other problems and risks!

Twenty sounds like an early age to begin such a dreadful process, and it is. This information has been gathered from studying large numbers of women of all ages and observing that the average 30-year-old woman has thinner bones than the average 20-year-old woman and that the average 40-year-old woman has even thinner bones, etc. This decline in average bone density is probably due largely to the adverse lifestyle practices listed above, especially inadequate dietary calcium and inadequate exercise.

Although osteoporosis is very common among older women, symptoms may not appear until the disease is very advanced. Sometimes low back and hip pain may be an early clue, but often the disease shows up first when a bone breaks. Many women get shorter as they get older, losing calcium from their vertebral bones. Constant pressure along these weakening bones often causes a marked curvature of the spine, colloquially known as "dowager's hump."

The Effect of Estrogen

After the menopause, women have much lower levels of estrogen than they did before. Since estrogen helps your bones to retain calcium, keeping them thick and strong, an estrogen deficiency promotes bone thinning. The high levels of estrogen a woman has before menopause prevent bone loss from occurring at a faster rate sooner. Women at high risk for developing osteoporosis probably should take estrogen, unless they have some reason not to. As we discussed in Chapter 6, women should not take estrogen if they have active liver disease, if they have had an undesirable blood clot (such as a heart attack, stroke, or thrombophlebitis—the clot that stops the bleeding when you cut your hand is a desirable blood clot), if they have had cancer of the breast or endometrium, or if they have unexplained vaginal bleeding. (The cause for such bleeding should be determined before any treatment is tried.)

Estrogen keeps calcium in your bones in several ways:

1. It enables your intestines to absorb more calcium from the foods you eat.
2. It prevents your bones from losing calcium so fast.
3. It makes your kidneys save more calcium too, by losing less in your urine.

Bone loss occurs pretty quickly during the first three years after the menopause. So you should not delay in doing something about it. Check with your doctor to see if you should be taking estrogen. If you should be, we recommend conjugated estrogens .625 milligrams daily on the first 25 days of every calendar month and medroxyprogesterone acetate 10 milligrams daily on days 16 through 25 of every calendar month.

The Importance of Exercise

Exercise is one of the few factors that directly helps to thicken your bones, by putting more calcium into them. (Most other factors that help to retard the process of bone thinning do so by preventing calcium from coming out of bones so fast.) Bones that bear weight are benefited the most. So walking won't thicken your arm bones, but lifting weights will.

When Sarah broke her hip last winter, everyone believed that she must have slipped on the ice and broken her hip when she hit the ground. Sarah didn't remember any ice, though, because there wasn't any. She fell down because she lost her balance when her hip broke from the ordinary forces of walking. That doesn't mean that walking is dangerous. It means that everything, including walking, is dangerous if you have thin bones. Exercise can help to strengthen your bones, and you'd better get started *before* your bones get thin.

The Importance of Calcium

Exercise will help to thicken and strengthen your bones only if you're getting enough calcium in your diet. After the menopause, you need 1,500 milligrams daily. To accomplish this, you'll have to consume a lot of dairy products, which are the best sources of calcium. Table 9-1

Table 9-1
GOOD SOURCES OF CALCIUM

Food	Portion Size	Calcium (mgm)	Calories
Skim milk	8 oz.	250	90
Whole milk	8 oz.	250	160
Yogurt (low fat fruit-flavored)	8 oz.	250	260
Cheddar cheese	1 oz.	250	100
Swiss cheese	1 oz.	250	100
Cottage cheese	10 oz.	250	300
Sardines with bones	3 oz.	250	300
Spinach, fresh or frozen	10 oz.	250	75

lists the amount of calcium in common foods, together with the number of calories. As you can see, the foods that will satisfy your calcium needs contain a lot of calories. For example, if you meet your daily calcium requirement of 1,500 milligrams by consuming two glasses of skim milk, two containers of yogurt, and two ounces of cheddar cheese, you'll have taken in 900 calories. Since the average sedentary woman burns up only about 1200-1400 calories per day, she has few allottable calories remaining with which to meet all of her other nutritional requirements. If you aren't exercising, you'll get fat if you eat enough of these foods to meet your calcium requirements.

Even if you are exercising (and we *hope* you are), you may not be able to tolerate enough of these foods because you may have a partial lactase deficiency. You require the enzyme lactase to degrade the milk sugar lactose into the simple sugars, glucose and galactose, of which it is made. If you lack lactase altogether, you cannot absorb lactose because it is a double sugar and only single sugars can be absorbed. Any unabsorbed lactose that enters your small intestine after you have eaten foods that contain it will pass undigested into your large intestine, where bacteria will ferment it, producing gas and diarrhea in the process. More than 50 percent of all people acquire a partial lactase deficiency as they get older, and they learn to limit their intake of dairy products to very small quantities.

If you aren't getting at least 1,500 milligrams of calcium in your daily diet, you probably should be taking supplementary calcium tablets to meet your needs. These can be purchased in almost any pharmacy, grocery store, or health food store in the form of calcium carbonate, calcium lactate, or calcium gluconate. (See Table 9-2.) Each calcium carbonate tablet contains 40 percent calcium, each calcium lactate tablet contains 12 percent calcium, and each calcium gluconate

Table 9-2
CALCIUM TABLETS

Calcium Salt	% Calcium	Tablet Size	Equivalent of 1 gram Calcium
Calcium carbonate	40%	600 mg.	4 tablets
Calcium gluconate	9%	600 mg.	18 tablets
Calcium lactate	13%	600 mg.	12 tablets

tablet contains 9 percent calcium. So it's a lot easier to meet your calcium needs with calcium carbonate than with any other preparation or diet alone. Although taking excessive amounts of most vitamins and minerals can be harmful to your body, taking excessive amounts of calcium (as much as 2,500 milligrams daily, for example) rarely causes any problems in healthy people. The only people who should *not* take calcium pills are those who have had kidney stones composed of calcium. These people have an increased risk of forming more calcium kidney stones. Since they shouldn't take calcium supplements and are as unlikely as most people to get enough calcium from the foods they eat, they are also at risk of developing osteoporosis. If you've passed the menopause, you probably need calcium supplements and should calculate what you are getting from your diet to be sure.

Other Ways to Treat Osteoporosis

Sodium fluoride helps to form bone and to retard its loss. Because of its high rate of side effects, it is much less helpful than might be expected. The major side effects that occur in people using it are stomach ulcers and bleeding, tendinitis, and joint pain.

Calcitonin slows down the rate at which calcium leaves your bones. Its side effects include mineral imbalance and allergic reactions from injections.

Anabolic steroids help to keep bones thick and strong, but these agents can lead to liver damage, hairiness, voice deepening, clitoral enlargement, acne, and male-pattern baldness. (See Chapter 3.)

Vitamin D in normal amounts is necessary to keep calcium in your bones, and you get a normal amount from eating a balanced diet and getting outdoors a bit. In excess, vitamin D may lead to liver damage and undesirable calcium deposits.

HEART DISEASE

Heart attacks are the leading cause of death in women over age 50. These are caused by coronary artery disease, in which the arteries supplying the heart become narrower and narrower and eventually close, as placques block them. A heart attack occurs when an artery closes and can't supply blood and oxygen to its portion of the muscle, which dies as a result.

Blocked coronary arteries occur with increasing age in both sexes, but much more commonly in men than in women. The discrepancy between men and women is partially due to hormones. The masculinizing hormone testosterone has an adverse effect on the ratio of high-density lipoprotein (HDL) cholesterol to low-density lipoprotein (LDL) cholesterol, while the feminizing hormone estrogen has a favorable effect on this ratio. This ratio is related to a lower risk of heart disease, meaning that a higher ratio carries a lower risk, and vice versa. After the menopause, women lose this protective effect of estrogen, and their risks rise then.

The age-related increase in coronary artery disease is also caused by many cumulative years of an adverse life-style, including too much dietary fat and too little exercise. Regular aerobic exercise lowers total blood cholesterol and raises the HDL/LDL ratio, thereby reducing the risk of coronary artery disease. Estrogen therapy leading to normal estrogen levels also raises this ratio and lowers cardiovascular risks. High doses of estrogen, on the other hand, promote clotting tendencies and raise cardiovascular risks. Thus, it is important to be taking the optimal dose if you are taking estrogen pills. Discuss this with your doctor, to be sure.

HOT FLUSHES

Seventy-five percent of all women experience hot flushes as they go through the menopause, and some women may have this discomforting problem for a year or even longer. These frequent heat waves are caused by a certain brain chemical that makes your blood vessels widen and your skin perspire. Doctors haven't identified the culprit yet. (Although many people refer to these uncomfortable sensations as "hot flashes," the correct term is really "hot flushes," since flashes are brief sensations of light, not warmth.)

Hot flushes can be very disabling, regardless of whether they occur while you're sleeping or awake. If they occur at night, they're likely to awaken you frequently, depriving you of precious sleep. Cumulative sleep loss can make most people irritable, and many menopausal women undergo undesirable changes in personality and behavior as a result of sleep deprivation caused by hot flushes. Such changes in personality usually make a woman irritable and short-tempered—the formerly accepted, but only recently explained, stereotypic picture of a menopausal woman.

Exercise, unfortunately, won't affect your hot flushes in any way, but estrogen therapy probably will. If you take estrogen to relieve hot flushes and for no other reason, you should take the lowest dose that will relieve the problem. In most cases, either .3 milligram or .625 milligram of conjugated estrogens daily will do the trick. Follow the same 25-day treatment schedule outlined on pages 118 and 146, adding medroxyprogesterone acetate on days 16 through 25 of every month.

VAGINAL DRYNESS

Vaginal dryness (atrophic vaginitis) is caused by a lack of estrogen, and the problem usually worsens the longer it lasts. Women who have this condition generally find it painful to have intercourse, but women who remain sexually active after the menopause are less likely to develop atrophic vaginitis. Apparently, repeated lubrication and stretching help to maintain the moistness and size of a normal vagina, while absence of these actions permit the vaginal wall to shrink and dry. So although sexual exercise can help to prevent this uncomfortable condition, it would be a painful way to treat it. Other types of exercise will have no effect on this condition.

OBESITY

Most people get fatter as they get older, and this problem is a bigger one for women than for men. Remember that the feminizing hormone estrogen promotes the formation of fat, while the masculinizing hormone testosterone promotes the formation of muscle. So sedentary women have a natural tendency to get fatter, while sedentary men do so at a much slower rate.

The main reason people get fatter is that they become progressively less active as they get older. Inactivity burns fewer calories and slows down metabolism too. If people remain as active in later years as in earlier ones, they do not get fatter and their rate of metabolism remains as high as before. Most people become less active for several reasons—social, cultural, and physical.

Older women, in particular, have been educated to be sedentary. Hopefully, this view is changing and will continue to change. Because muscles, tendons, and ligaments lose elasticity with increasing age, most people avoid exercise to avoid athletic injury. This is an unnecessary and unhealthful avoidance, in fact. Proper exercise will lead to many benefits and reduce many risks.

The same rules of fitness apply to older and younger people. Since it takes longer for their muscles to recover from exercise, older people should practice different sports on alternate days or should exercise only on alternate days. The rule of listening to your body applies to everyone, young and old.

Obesity is associated with increased risks of several medical problems, including diabetes mellitus, high blood pressure, coronary artery disease, and certain cancers. If regular exercise prevents you from becoming obese, you will be less likely to develop any of these problems. You'll also be happier about your trim, slim body. (Refer to Chapter 1 to review how exercise avoids fat accumulation by speeding up your metabolism and burning a lot more calories.)

DEPRESSION

Depression is a common problem among older people of both sexes, probably because the brain concentrations of mood-elevating chemicals often decline with increasing age. The major causes of depression include several social factors, such as loneliness, isolation, dependency, disability, illness, death of loved ones, end of work life, lack of physical affection, and lack of being needed. In addition to all of these changes, the menopause itself can promote depression. As we discussed before, cumulative sleep deprivation from frequent hot flushes can lead to psychological problems such as irritability, and it can cause depression too. Estrogen can improve sleep that is disrupted by hot flushes, and this will relieve the depression too.

Of course, depression is rarely caused by hot flushes and sleep deprivation. Since depression often disrupts sleep, it may be very difficult to determine cause and effect. If you think you are depressed, having blue feelings and frequent crying spells, check with a psychologist or psychiatrist, who are the specialists most likely to help you. As we've mentioned before, intelligent, educated people are most likely to benefit from consultation with one of these professionals. Understanding the problem may help to correct it. Your doctor will help you decide whether medication will be helpful too.

Exercise too can prevent or treat depression, probably in several ways. Exercise helps your brain produce more mood-elevating chemicals and also helps you feel better about your attractive, fit body.

Being slim and trim gives most people a psychological boost. This high is so strong that it hooks many people on regular exercise. Most older people need this lift even more than younger ones do.

EXERCISE CAUTIONS FOR OLDER WOMEN

If you are in good health and have no discomfort when you exercise, you probably don't need any special examinations or tests to determine whether you can exercise safely. On the other hand, light-headedness, chest pain, and excessive shortness of breath during exercise are signs that something is wrong. These symptoms should always be checked and may indicate diseases that require supervised or curtailed exercises.

Doctors once recommended that everyone over age 40 be checked by a doctor before beginning an exercise program. This checkup was supposed to include an examination and an exercise cardiogram (measurement of the heart's electrical function during exercise). Studies have shown that exercise cardiograms rarely detect abnormalities in people who have no symptoms such as light-headedness, chest or neck pain, or excessive shortness of breath. Thus, this most common evaluation of heart health is recommended only for those who have symptoms of disease.

GUIDELINES

If you are over age 40 or even over age 70, you should follow the same guidelines for each type of fitness recommended for younger people. (See Chapter 1.) Pain is always an indicator that something is wrong, and you should avoid any exercise that causes pain.

Recommended Sports

The best sports for older women are brisk walking, stationary bicycling, and swimming. Each of these can be practiced at your target heart rate and will strengthen your heart, your muscles, and your bones. Jogging usually is *not* a good sport for older people because they are more likely to be injured in this sport, and injuries often lead to avoidance of beneficial exercise. When your foot strikes the ground

Table 9-3
RECOMMENDED SPORTS FOR OLDER WOMEN

Brisk walking	Jogging on trampoline
Stationary bicycling	Calisthenics
Swimming	Weight training
Ping-Pong	Square dancing
Water calisthenics	Rowing (on machine)

in brisk walking, it lands with your body weight. When your foot strikes the ground during jogging, it lands with three times your body weight, a force that often injures older bones, muscles, tendons, ligaments, and joints. For this reason, walking is a much safer sport than jogging for most older people who have never jogged before. Many older people who are accustomed to jogging are familiar enough with their bodies and its signals that they are less likely to be injured because they know when to stop. Neophytes are often less familiar with these subtle body cues and may be injured too soon or too often to reap the rewards of exercise. Because a trampoline absorbs a great portion of the shock when your foot strikes it, jogging on a trampoline is very safe, even for older people.

Calisthenics will promote flexibility, and weight lifting will promote muscle strength. Thus, these are excellent choices for older as well as younger women.

Table 9-3 shows sports that promote fitness, while Table 9-4 shows sports that are safe but not directed toward physical improvement. Aerobic dancing, although excellent for younger women, may be too fast and dangerous for older women trying to keep pace with them. Square dancing, however, uses less whole-body motion and tends to be slower and safer for older women.

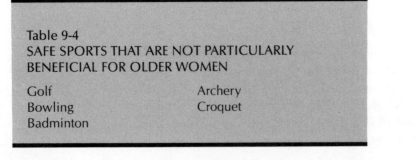

Table 9-4
SAFE SPORTS THAT ARE NOT PARTICULARLY
BENEFICIAL FOR OLDER WOMEN

Golf	Archery
Bowling	Croquet
Badminton	

10 SPECIAL GYNECOLOGIC CONCERNS

Several gynecologic conditions concern nearly all women, irrespective of their athletic participation. However, execise may affect or be affected by these conditions. So athletes may, at times, need special advice.

CONTRACEPTION

If you practice sexual intercourse with a male partner and have semen deposited in your vagina, you probably should be using a contraceptive agent unless you are trying to become pregnant now. The only exceptions to this are women of any age who have passed the menopause, since their ovaries have run out of functioning eggs. If you have any other problem that has disrupted regular menstruation, you should still be practicing contraception because most other problems could resolve spontaneously without warning, possibly leaving you with an unwanted and unexpected pregnancy. As we discussed in Chapter 6, amenorrheic athletes, after thorough evaluation, should use contraception if they don't want to become pregnant. For these women, birth control pills offer skeletal and endometrial protection in addition to contraceptive efficacy.

Your choice of the optimal contraceptive agent is rarely affected by the fact that you exercise. It should take into consideration many other factors, such as your age, whether you smoke, your childbearing plans, sexual pattern, and medical problems. The overall effectiveness of contraceptives is shown in Table 10-1.

Table 10-1
CONTRACEPTIVE FAILURE RATES DURING FIRST YEAR
OF USE
(per 100 married women aged 15 to 44 including
correct and incorrect use)

Birth control pill	2
Intrauterine device	4
Condom	10
Diaphragm	13
Foam, cream, or jelly	15
Rhythm	19

Birth Control Pills

Birth control pills contain both estrogen and progesterone derivatives in higher concentrations than your body produces naturally. (A "progestin" is a hormone structurally similar to pure progesterone, which is made naturally by your body. Synthetic progesterone and natural progesterone are both progestins.) These higher concentrations of estrogen and progesterone derivatives suppress the production of the brain hormones that stimulate your ovaries to make their own estrogen and progesterone and stimulate the growth and development of an egg within the ovary. As a result, birth control pills usually prevent ovulation, so that pregnancy is very unlikely to occur while you are taking them. The progestin in birth control pills also makes your cervical mucus thick, sticky, scanty, and thereby hostile to sperm. In addition, the progestin in these pills interferes with the normal muscular contractions of the Fallopian tubes and the motions of the hairlike cilia that line these tubes, also making it harder for the egg to travel through your tube into your uterus if you do ovulate.

If you do not smoke cigarettes, low-dose birth control pills (each containing 30 to 35 micrograms of estrogen and an appropriate amount of a progestin) are probably a very safe contraceptive choice for you. The usual taboos exist for estrogen, of course, as discussed in Chapters 6 and 9. Thus, you shouldn't take birth control pills if you have active liver disease, if you have ever had an undesirable blood clot (a heart attack, a stroke, or thrombophlebitis), or if you have had breast or endometrial cancer. If you smoke cigarettes, or if you have a hereditary condition causing high blood fat levels, birth control pills convey a slight risk of undesirable blood clots, particularly if you are over age 35. You should consider another form of contraception if you fall into this category.

Birth control pills offer many benefits, in addition to their high success rate as contraceptive agents. Women have less menstrual blood loss while taking them and, therefore, lose less iron. So birth control pills help to prevent iron deficiency and anemia. Because they are taken on a regular schedule that is unrelated to sexual activity, they do not interfere with the spontaneity of lovemaking.

Since estrogen helps to keep calcium in your bones, birth control pills will also help to prevent osteoporosis. Scientific studies have also shown that women taking birth control pills are less likely to develop pelvic infections (internal infections involving the Fallopian tubes and ovaries), although they are more likely to develop vaginal infections, which are much less serious. So birth control pills offer many advantages in addition to their contraceptive efficacy.

Intrauterine Devices

Intrauterine devices (IUDs) are objects that are inserted into your uterus by a professional (usually by a doctor). They may be "active" (containing a chemical that adds to the contraceptive action) or "inert" (containing no chemicals). They prevent pregnancies by keeping the fertilized egg from settling comfortably in the uterus. These agents are good contraceptives for women who have completed their families, particularly if they have intercourse at least twice a week and have any reason to avoid birth control pills. Like birth control pills, they do not interfere with the spontaneity of lovemaking.

IUDs impose a slight risk of pelvic infections, some of which may lead to infertility (inability to get pregnant when you want to). Thus, we do not recommend IUDs for women who plan to have children, regardless of whether they already have any.

Although IUDs are quite effective in preventing pregnancies from occurring in the uterus, they are not without risk. IUD-wearers have a higher chance than those using other contraceptive methods of having pregnancies in their Fallopian tubes. Tubal pregnancies can rupture and lead to much internal blood loss, and even death if not treated in time.

Those who get pregnant while using an IUD have an increased

risk of developing a serious pelvic infection that can endanger both mother and fetus.

Some women who have IUDs experience more menstrual cramps and bleeding than usual. Since pain and bleeding can inconvenience an athlete, you may want to switch to another contraceptive method if you have either of these IUD-related problems.

Women who have IUDs tend to lose more menstrual blood, as a result of which they are more likely to become iron-deficient and even anemic. Less menstrual blood loss occurs with IUDs containing copper or progesterone than with most other types. Since iron deficiency or anemia can impair the performance of an athlete, you may want to select a device containing progesterone or copper if the IUD is the optimal contraceptive for you.

Barrier Contraception

Barrier methods of contraception include the diaphragm, the sponge, foams, jellies, and condoms. These agents prevent pregnancy by impeding the union of egg and sperm. Studies have shown that more athletes use barrier methods of contraception than any other type, and the diaphragm seems preferred more than other methods. It is not surprising that athletes favor methods requiring the same self-discipline and motivation that characterize other aspects of their lives. Those with less discipline are unable to use these agents as effectively. Since athletes often prefer "natural" ways of living, it is likely that they prefer barrier methods of contraception also because these methods do not disrupt natural body functions.

To provide optimal contraception, the diaphragm should be covered with contraceptive jelly and should be inserted into your vagina no more than one hour before ejaculation takes place. It should remain in place in your vagina for at least six hours after ejaculation. If more than one ejaculation occurs during this time, additional foam or jelly should be inserted into your vagina (without removing the diaphragm) before each subsequent ejaculation takes place. It is alright to exercise (in any sport) while your diaphragm is still in place. If you experience any discomfort when you do so, ask your gynecologist to prescribe a diaphragm one size smaller. This will probably provide greater comfort without reducing contraceptive efficacy.

Foams and jellies kill or immobilize sperm, so that the sperm can't reach the egg to fertilize it. These agents are safe and convenient, although rather messy. As applies to their use with a diaphragm, they should be inserted no longer than one hour before ejaculation and should remain in place in your vagina at least six hours after ejaculation. Additional foam or jelly should be inserted prior to any subsequent ejaculations. Although foams and jellies can be used alone, they are far more effective when used in combination with a diaphragm or condom.

These agents are a fine choice for all athletes. For women who have intercourse less frequently than twice a week, they may actually be preferred. However, their messiness and subsequent leakage may make them somewhat less desirable for active athletes. For example, you may notice that some of the jelly or foam you inserted for intercourse leaks out while you're running afterward. This nuisance can usually be remedied by wearing a tampon or mini-pad.

A condom also serves as a barrier to the union of sperm and egg. It is a rubber sheath that is placed on an erect penis before ejaculation occurs. It remains on the penis until after the penis has been removed from the vagina. Its major advantages are convenience, availability, and reduction of disease transmission. Its major disadvantage is that it requires disruption of lovemaking during excitement in order to apply the condom. Of course, if you apply the condom to your male partner (rather than have him apply it himself), your application may actually enhance his sexual excitement! Like the diaphragm, the condom requires a bit of practice before it can be used comfortably and effectively. First-time users generally feel quite clumsy while putting it on, and all condom users must be careful that the condom remains in place as the penis is removed. If the condom rolls up or falls off as the penis is withdrawn, sperm will end up in the vagina, despite all heroic efforts to avoid this.

The sponge is a relatively new method of barrier contraception. Because of its newness, the sponge hasn't been tested or studied as much as other contraceptive agents, and as a result, we know much less about how safe and effective it is. One type of sponge is made up of a soft polyurethane material that releases a spermicidal agent slowly and continuously. This type may be left in your vagina for 24-48 hours, and it should be left in place for at least six hours after the last ejaculation has taken place (as is true for other spermicidal agents too). Another type is made of a fiber-like mesh that is placed into the top of your vagina, where it traps sperm. This type may be left in place for several days. Because a sponge may be left in place so long, it offers an advantage in that its use doesn't disrupt lovemaking. Aside from some infrequent reactions to the chemicals it contains, its only major disadvantage is its newness and consequent lack of being proven by numerous scientific tests.

STRESS URINARY INCONTINENCE

Stress urinary incontinence refers to involuntary urine leakage during any stress which raises the internal abdominal pressure. This pressure rises during actions like coughing, sneezing, laughing, and most exercises that involve jumping or straining. You are most likely to lose urine involuntarily if you have a dropped (prolapsed) uterus or dropped bladder. Both of these conditions are more likely to occur in women who have given birth several times, since the stretching of pelvic tissues and attaching supports during childbirth may cause such dropping to occur.

Exercise does not cause or worsen these anatomic abnormalities, but women who already have either of these conditions will be more likely to experience leakage when they exercise than when they rest, due to the internal pressure increase during exercise. So exercise increases the symptoms but doesn't worsen the condition.

Many other conditions can cause involuntary urine leakage too, such as a stretched and insensitive bladder, an irritable bladder, or an infected bladder. If you leak urine uncontrollably, consult a gynecologist or urologist to determine the cause. You'll need some special tests, including one in which your bladder pressure is measured (cystometry), one in which your bladder is X-rayed with dye inside it (cystography), and two in which your urine is checked for an infection (urinalysis and culture). Once the cause for the problem has been found, you can probably be treated to get partial or complete improvement.

If a dropped uterus or dropped bladder is responsible for your urine leakage, your doctor may suggest an operation to return the dropped organ to its proper position. First, though, there are several helpful things you can and should do:

1. Always empty your bladder just before you exercise. This will minimize any urine leakage during exercise, particularly since your bladder won't accumulate very much urine while you're exercising.
2. Practice Kegel exercises, in which you alternately contract and relax the muscles around your vagina, to help strengthen them.

You can identify the right muscles by placing a finger just inside the opening of your vagina and squeezing that finger with the muscles around your vagina. Once you've practiced it with your finger, you'll be able to do it without any aids. Kegel exercises may strengthen your outer vaginal muscles enough so that you can control your urine satisfactorily.

3. Wear a mini-pad when you exercise to handle any accidents.

Don't let this embarrassing problem prevent you from exercising. If you have an operation to correct the problem, you should be able to resume exercising within two months, and hopefully you'll be free from the chagrin you faced before.

INFECTIONS

Vaginitis

Vaginitis is an infection of the vagina, and it is usually caused by one of three organisms: *Candida vaginalis, Trichomonas vaginalis,* or *Gardnerella vaginalis.* The most common symptoms caused by any of these infections are vaginal itching, discharge, and odor. Exercise doesn't cause any of these infections, but the discomfort of vaginitis can interfere with your exercise.

If you have any of these symptoms, consult your gynecologist, who will do a "wet prep" examination in which he or she will examine your vaginal discharge through a microscope. This will uncover the responsible organism, and you can then be treated with appropriate medication.

Several old myths claimed that moist, tight underclothes made women more susceptible to developing vaginitis. There are no scientific studies to support this claim, and your underwear has nothing to do with the condition. Your vagina is normally moist anyway, and moist or tight underwear has no effect on the moistness of your vagina.

Candida is a yeast infection and usually causes itching. Certain women are particularly susceptible to this. For example, women taking birth control pills or antibiotics, pregnant women, and diabetics are more likely to acquire this type of infection. Candida grows in a high-sugar environment. Diabetics tend to have more sugar in all their cells, including the cells of their vaginas. Pregnant women and women taking birth control pills have high levels of estrogen and progesterone, which raise the sugar content in the cells of the vagina. Antibiotics that kill harmful bacteria causing infections anywhere in your body also kill the good bacteria that normally live in your vagina, thus permitting and promoting the growth of Candida and other harmful fungi. If you tend to get this infection frequently and aren't in one of these categories, your doctor may want to check to see if your immunity is abnormal. If you get Candida vaginitis only when you take antibiotics, you can use medicated suppositories whenever you take antibiotics, in order to prevent future vaginitis of this type. This disease can be transmitted sexually, but very rarely is.

Trichomonas usually causes a very profuse discharge, generally having a pungent odor. This infection is transmitted sexually and your sexual partner should be treated too. If you have intercourse with more than one male, all should be treated in order to eradicate the infection. Treatment involves taking metronidazole tablets, preferably for a few days. You can probably get this infection from a contaminated toilet seat, tub, whirlpool, towel, or cloth too (although these modes of transmission are rather uncommon), so choose your health club wisely! (See Chapter 12 for a discussion of a skin disease you can acquire in a whirlpool.)

Gardnerella usually causes a very sharp odor, with or without a discharge. This can be transmitted sexually too, and your male partner or partners should be treated with antibiotics at the same time you are. You probably can also acquire this infection from a contaminated toilet seat, tub, whirlpool, cloth, or towel, if wet, although much less commonly than by sexual transmission.

Herpes

Herpes is a virus that can infect your vulva (your outer genital area), your cervix (the mouth of your uterus), your bladder, and your urethra (the tube that drains your bladder). To get this infection, you must have an open sore, which must be rubbed with the virus. So you can get this infection during intercourse from an infected male partner, but you'd be much less likely to get it by sitting on a contaminated health club towel because friction would be lacking.

Because herpes sores can cause excruciating pain, this infection can make it uncomfortable to exercise, particularly if your sport involves sitting. There is no medical reason to avoid exercise when you have an active herpes infection, but the pain will probably preclude exercise while you have painful blisters. You don't have to worry about getting herpes from an infected person swimming in your pool, unless your skin rubs against the active herpes sores while you are swimming. Doctors still await a cure for herpes. Until one is found, the viral disease must take its own time to resolve, usually 4 to 14 days.

Internal Pelvic Infections

Infections that involve your vagina, cervix, or vulva usually cause external symptoms. Except for herpes, these rarely interfere with your training. Internal infections, on the other hand, can cause debilitating internal pain in your lower belly, and this can preclude exercising for a while.

Internal infections of your pelvic organs may involve your uterus, Fallopian tubes, and ovaries. Such infections usually cause fever and abdominal pain. These infections can be caused by many bacteria, including the gonococcus, which causes gonorrhea. When this organism infects the cervix, victims usually have no symptoms, except for a possible discharge. However, the gonococcus can pass from the cervix through the uterus and into the Fallopian tubes, where the infection can cause severe abdominal pain. Because it's hard to exercise with pain, pain anywhere can interfere with training and competition. Internal pelvic infections can cause infertility too, by blocking and scarring the Fallopian tubes. Powerful intravenous antibiotics are usually required to treat such infections, and you'll have to postpone your training until the pain is gone and intravenous treatment is completed. This may take as long as two or three weeks.

Always remember that pain is an indication that something is wrong. Abdominal pain and fever probably mean that you have an internal infection, and you'll be wise to be evaluated promptly, so that you can be treated promptly too.

INFERTILITY

Infertility is the inability to achieve a pregnancy when desired. Studies have shown that athletes have the same prevalence of infertility as that found among the general population, even though they are more likely to have irregular periods and amenorrhea, which can cause infertility. Why, then, do athletes not have a higher prevalence of infertility than the general population? Perhaps it is because most athletes who are training seriously are not trying to become pregnant and are not, thus, technically infertile, even though they might be unable to become pregnant if they were to try.

Athletes are no more susceptible to most causes of infertility than the general population. However, they are more susceptible to luteal phase defects and lack of ovulation, both of which can cause infertility. Both of these conditions can be treated with medication, so most athletes can probably become pregnant, although some will need treatment to do so.

Some infertile athletes may prefer to (1) stop exercising; (2) reduce exercise intensity, frequency, or duration; or (3) gain weight or fat as a trial before taking medication. These are acceptable options. If you choose any of these plans and it works for you—fine! If you prefer to continue training as you have been, though, it is equally fine to take medication and keep exercising. Only you can decide which plan is best for you.

If you are trying to get pregnant and are unable to do so, consult an infertility specialist (usually a reproductive endocrinologist) for a thorough evaluation of you, your partner, and the interaction between the two of you. Most infertility problems have nothing to do with exercise.

ENDOMETRIOSIS

Endometriosis is a condition in which pieces of the inner lining of the uterus are located outside the uterus. Althouth many women who have this disorder have no symptoms at all, many experience pain, infertility, or both. The lower abdominal pain that results from endometriosis usually begins several days before the beginning of your menstrual period and lasts for several days, perhaps even during most of the period too. This is quite different from normal menstrual cramps, which rarely begin more than a day before your period begins.

The diagnosis of endometriosis should be based on more than just pain or infertility. Before deciding that you have this condition, you should have a procedure called a laparoscopy, in which your doctor looks inside your abdomen through a lighted tube. If your doctor, while looking inside, has any question about whether you actually have endometriosis, he or she should remove a small piece of the abnormal tissue (a procedure called a biopsy) and examine it through a microscope.

Depending upon the severity of the disease and its symptoms, treatment can vary. Some women need an operation, some need medication, and some require no treatment at all. While some women may be treated with either birth control pills or medroxyprogesterone acetate, the most effective drug used to treat endometriosis today is danazol, an anabolic steroid. (See Chapter 3 for our discussion of anabolic steroids.) Some athletes who are taking this drug to treat endometriosis notice increased motivation to train, and some report greater strength. However, there are no scientific studies of athletic performance in women using this agent. As an anabolic steroid, this medication will be detected by drug tests for anabolic steroids. Thus, competitive athletes who have endometriosis should consider the merits and risks of taking this drug for gynecologic reasons when they are seriously competing. Discuss the pros and cons with your gynecologist.

11 CHOOSING THE RIGHT UNDERWEAR AND SWIMWEAR

There are no medical reasons why you have to wear underwear. The only purpose of underwear is to provide comfort. In hot weather, it should keep you cool. In cool weather, it should keep you warm. If it hurts to have parts of your body bouncing around, your underwear should keep them still. If your underwear makes you uncomfortable, it is worthless and you should get rid of it.

Women of different sizes and shapes and participating in different sports need different types of underwear. No one garment is ideal for all women in all situations. The lacy, seductive bra that is appropriate for a secluded candle-lit dinner with your lover is as unsuitable for running as your downhill ski boots are for the candle-lit dinner with your lover. Just as you need the right equipment for any specialized activity, you need the right underwear too.

YOUR BREASTS

Breast Comfort

The right bra should be loose enough to let you breathe and move freely and tight enough to keep your breasts from bouncing. Most large-breasted women find it more comfortable to exercise while wearing a bra that provides good support, but many small-breasted women find greater comfort exercising without a bra. Averagebreasted women usually prefer bras with moderate support. There is no medical reason why you have to wear a bra; your own comfort should guide you.

Although large breasts may bounce uncomfortably during running or basketball, your chest and arms may lift weights more comfortably if you are braless. Both physical and psychological comfort must be considered, though. The physical comfort of weight lifting braless may be matched by psychological comfort when you are in the privacy of your own home, but may be surpassed by psychological *discomfort* when you are in a crowded health club with a lot of attentive eyes watching you. No "perfect" bra exists for all women or for all activities. You must try on any bra and move around in it. It's difficult to play basketball or volleyball in the fitting room of a busy department store, but you should simulate the movements of your sport there as well as you can—even if you have an audience! Embarrassment in the store is less painful than an uncomfortable bra on the tennis court afterward!

Although the ideal bra doesn't exist, many comfortable ones provide good support for sports. Avoid those that ride up or twist, those that have bones or wires that dig into your body, those loose enough to slide and rub your skin, and those that have seams that rub your skin or hooks that dig into your skin. Keep looking until you find a suitable one, and remember that you may need different bras for different sports. If your breasts become larger or painful before your period, you may need a larger or more supportive bra for that time of the month.

Breast Size and Shape

Your breasts are made up mostly of fat tissue. Since they contain no muscles, exercise will not enlarge or reduce actual breast size. Of course, any aerobic sports that lead to an overall loss of body fat will lead to some fat loss from your breasts too. Since your breasts are composed of mostly fat, any loss of breast fat will reduce breast size. Similarly, getting fatter will make your breasts fatter and larger too. So the only way to enlarge your breasts is by getting fatter, and the only way to reduce your breasts is by getting thinner. Exercises that strengthen your chest muscles may give the illusion of a fuller chest, but your actual breast size will be the same.

Although fat women tend to have larger breasts and thin women smaller breasts, breast size and body fat distribution are also determined partly by heredity. That is why large-breasted women tend to have large-breasted mothers and daughters. (Similarly, women with fat thighs tend to have mothers and daughters with fat thighs.) Of course, thin women *can* have large breasts, and fat women can have small breasts, since total body fat content is not the only determinant of breast size. However, large-breasted thin women and small-breasted fat women are the exception, rather than the rule.

The relationship between body fat and breast size applies to mature women who have fairly regular periods. Those who have amenorrhea and low estrogen levels may have inadequate breast development from their estrogen deficiency. These women can enlarge their breasts by taking estrogen to replace what their bodies are not making. (Of course, they need a thorough evaluation first, as we've already discussed in Chapter 6.) However, hormonal supplements will not alter breast size noticeably in women who menstruate at least as often as once every three months, for these women can be presumed to have normal estrogen levels.

Exercising alone will not cause your breasts to sag. Breast sagging occurs in all women as they get older, and the tendency to develop sagging earlier is inherited somewhat too. Large, heavy breasts are more likely to sag because this heavy weight stretches the skin covering them as they hang downward. If any exercise makes heavy breasts bounce, it can increase this stretching with every bounce and, hence, hasten this sagging too. So it's the weight of heavy breasts that makes them sag, not exercise. Although the decision to wear a bra remains a matter of personal comfort, we recommend supportive bras for large-breasted women during exercise and routine activities too.

If the size of your breasts is out of proportion to your overall body composition and is disturbing you psychologically, you may want to consider an operation to enlarge or reduce your breasts. Such operations, called augmentation mammoplasty and reduction mammoplasty respectively, are performed by plastic surgeons. Discuss this with your doctor if you think such an operation may help you.

PANTIES

The only rule for selecting panties is comfort. Nothing else matters. Panties that constrict you, rub you, ride up, slip down, or overheat you are undesirable. Because cotton absorbs moisture and permits it to evaporate, cotton panties may offer an advantage for exercises that cause perspiration. As we discussed in Chapter 10, panties of materials other than cotton do not make women more susceptible to infections, despite some old myths to the contrary. Although cotton panties provide comfort by absorbing moisture, many synthetic fibers offer even more comfort by staying in place well. The elasticity of many nylon stretch fabrics may provide more comfort than ordinary cotton panties for vigorous activity, but cotton panties of elastic stretch fabrics may be most comfortable, and many athletes prefer them. Personal comfort must guide you here. Some synthetic fabrics, such as polypropylene, offer greatest comfort. These draw any moisture away from your skin toward the outer surface of the fabric, from where it can evaporate. Some of these stay in place well too.

Many athletes find polypropylene underwear to be quite durable, but some report that it retains an unpleasant odor despite frequent washings, and some find it requires delicate washing care, a time-consuming nuisance for women on the go.

Most running shorts are made with built-in panties, usually with a cotton crotch. These are so comfortable and fit so well that no underwear is needed.

If your sport is cycling, you'll probably need chamois-crotch panties, which prevent friction against your delicate genital skin. Such friction could rub away at your outer lips and surrounding structures, leaving you too sore to sit on a bicycle seat again. Chamois, which is a soft leather made from various skins dressed with fish oil, is rough on the outer side and smooth on the inner side. The rough side faces the bicycle seat, preventing movement, and the smooth side faces your underwear or skin, permitting sliding without rubbing.

GIRDLES AND CORSETS

Many women grew up in an era of girdles and corsets—restricting garments that bound their torsos into the shapes and sizes desired. Such garments are uncomfortable, unhealthful, and even dangerous. A corset can act as a tourniquet for your legs, making it harder for your leg veins to return blood to your heart and causing your legs to swell from the constriction. As uncomfortable as it is to sit or stand in a girdle, it is even more uncomfortable to move in one, making exercise nearly impossible. If you grew up thinking that tidy, attractive women should wear girdles, or if you believe your clothes look better when you squeeze your fat into a girdle underneath, you should be exercising to change your body rather than suffering to hide it. A loose-fitting sweat suit will feel marvelous as you practice aerobic dancing or jogging in place in the privacy of your own home. After you shed some of your fat, you'll be ready to invest in some loose-fitting panties that are pretty too. In any event, get rid of your girdles. They won't let you exercise at all.

LEOTARDS AND TIGHTS

Leotards are snug-fitting knitted garments that cover your body from neck to torso, available in both short-sleeved and long-sleeved versions. Tights are snug-fitting knitted garments that cover your legs from ankles or toes to waist.

Many health clubs and exercise classes require you to wear leotards and tights in order to participate. There is no medical or health reason for this requirement, and there are several reasons against it. Leotards and tights offer most women a colorful and curvaceous look, and their elasticity helps to camouflage some fat lumps too. In cold weather, they can provide welcome warmth, but this is not the environment in which they are required. It is indoors that they must be worn, where it is already warm and where you will become even warmer while exercising. You certainly don't need elastic garments hugging most of your skin to make you even warmer. Wearing leotards and tights increases your likelihood of overheating, which can reduce your safe exercise limit or make you ill. (See Chapter 4 for our discussion of heat illnesses.) Leotards and tights shouldn't be outlawed, but their use should certainly be optional—desirable in cold weather, generally undesirable in warm weather.

If you are embarrassed by the fat jiggling on your upper thighs as you run, tights are a rather safe and comfortable way to conceal this unsightly weight, as long as the ambient temperature is 65 degrees Fahrenheit or less. At higher temperatures, it can be dangerous to exercise vigorously in tights and leotards. Looser, lighter fabrics will be much more comfortable and much safer too.

SANITARY PROTECTION

Your choice for sanitary protection depends on your own comfort. Both sanitary napkins (or pads) and tampons offer advantages for different situations. Most athletes prefer tampons, though, because internal protection is more comfortable, more convenient, and less visible.

Tampons are absorbent products that you insert into your vagina, where they absorb menstrual blood before it has a chance to reach the outside. Sanitary napkins are worn in the crotch of your panties, where they absorb menstrual blood as soon as it leaves your vagina. A sanitary napkin stays in place best when your legs are stationary and together, so any vigorous leg movements can cause the pad to slip and permit blood to escape onto your underwear or outerwear. Such napkin slippage can also irritate your skin and create the same annoying feeling you get when your underpants ride up or slip down. A tampon will remain in place no matter what your legs are doing, so tampon use will give your legs much more freedom of movement.

For any water sport, you'll have to wear a tampon because an external pad would act like a sponge, absorbing pool or ocean water as well as your menstrual blood. This mixture of blood and water would be squeezed out onto your swimsuit and into the pool or ocean water, leaving a telltale trail behind you. Since your vagina remains closed around a tampon, and since the tampon is absorbing the menstrual blood while it is still in your vagina, under ordinary circumstances no blood should leak out from your vagina while a tampon is inside.

However, most women have experienced leakage around or through a tampon. Such accidents are fairly uncommon except for those who menstruate very heavily. Heavy periods (discussed in Chapter 6) usually require super tampons or tampons and pads worn simultaneously. If you have this problem, you may want to avoid swimming on the days you menstruate most heavily. Tassette cups, which were rubber cups designed to fit snugly over the cervix and hold menstrual blood, are no longer manufactured. These had offered the best alternative for heavy menstruation and inaccessibility to changing tampons frequently, and it is unfortunate that they are no longer manufactured.

Discuss heavy menstrual flow with your gynecologist if you are a competitive swimmer, for you'll probably need treatment to reduce your flow so that you won't have to disrupt your training.

A few years ago, toxic shock syndrome (TSS) scared some women away from tampon use. Scientific studies have revealed that this very rare disease is caused by a toxin produced by bacteria, which can grow more easily in the aerated environment created by a vaginal tampon. Tampons do not cause this rare disease, and athletes should not be afraid to use tampons unless they have already had toxic shock syndrome. Women who have had TSS have an increased risk of having it again and should probably avoid tampon use, in order to decrease this risk. Competitive athletes who have had TSS and who require tampons in order to continue training and competing should ask their gynecologists to prescribe antibiotics to decrease their risks of getting TSS again. This may enable them to continue using tampons. Discuss this with your own doctor if you face this dilemma.

SWIMWEAR

Swimwear should be like underwear: comfortable. However, bathing suits are designed for both function and appearance. Some make your body look beautiful, but may fall off or ride up if you try to swim in them. Others permit you to swim comfortably, but reveal lumps and bulges you never saw before. If you can find a bathing suit that both fits and flatters, you are very fortunate.

Ideally, a bathing suit should reveal your more attractive parts, conceal your less attractive parts, stretch when you move, and remain in place always. It should have no seams that rub you, no tight elastic that binds you, no straps that fall down, and no bones, wires, or hooks that dig into your skin. Very few bathing suit manufacturers offer separate chest and cup sizes. Roxanne is the only manufacturer we could find that is currently offering swimwear in specific cup sizes.

Since women vary greatly in their proportions, it is extremely difficult to find a suit that fits perfectly in all places. Bathing suits *should* include four sizes: chest circumference, breast (cup) size, hip circumference, and length (either shoulder to crotch or breast to crotch). None do. Two-piece suits obviously do not need a length measurement and are thus easier to fit into. However, most two-piece suits are offered in only one size for top and bottom, disregarding cup size altogether. Because most companies offer standard sizes for nonstandard bodies, most women either wear poorly fitting suits or else avoid swimming. Hopefully, more companies will manufacture suits with more specific sizes for each important dimension. Until this happens, though, plan to shop around until you can find the suit offering the best compromise between fit and appearance.

Other options include finding a good dressmaker to create one that fits you properly, sewing a suit yourself (if you're skillful enough with needle and thread), and wearing the attractive leotard that is too warm for your exercise class!

SUPPORT HOSE

Normal, healthy people do not need support hose for sports. Such hose compress the superficial veins in your legs and help to return the blood to your heart. When you exercise your legs, your leg muscles contract, pumping the blood to your heart more effectively than support hose can possibly do it.

The only time healthy people really need support hose is while standing still for a long time, particularly if their jobs require them to do so frequently. If your job includes a lot of walking, the exercise will push the blood toward your heart. On the other hand, if your job includes a lot of standing in one place (for example, if you are a surgeon, an operating room scrub nurse, or a supermarket cashier), the blood will tend to collect in the superficial veins of your legs, and this can make your legs swell and ache. Support hose can prevent this swelling and aching.

Support hose can be helpful for women who have varicose veins (discussed in Chapter 13), but normal women do not need support hose. However, support hose are very comfortable, and many women prefer to wear them for this reason alone.

SOCKS

Most athletes wear socks for comfort. If your shoes were molded perfectly around your feet, socks would be needed only to collect the dead cells and dirt rubbed off from your feet, so that your shoes would be spared from such debris and the odor it causes as bacteria degrade them. Shoes do not fit perfectly, though, and socks are needed to fill the empty spaces so that your shoes will fit better. Socks also prevent friction from any rough spots in your shoes rubbing against your feet. Such friction can cause painful blisters, which can make it uncomfortable for you to exercise. The softest materials make the most comfortable socks. Since cotton absorbs moisture, it offers an additional advantage. Wool, too, absorbs moisture and retains heat even while wet. Although wet cotton socks may be uncomfortably cold in cold weather, wet woolen socks will probably keep you warm.

If your sport involves high shoes or boots, choose socks that extend above them. One of the most common places where blisters arise is at the top of your shoes, for this edge frequently rubs against your skin during exercise. As a general rule, your socks should usually extend higher than your shoe tops. Many women prefer low golf socks, which extend minimally above the top of a standard shoe and which often have a pom-pom at the back of the top, preventing the sock from slipping down into your shoe. These are often made of terry cloth, which is soft, comfortable, and absorbent, although it frequently stiffens after much wear, perspiration, and washing.

As with all underwear, you should find a pair of comfortable socks and replace them with the same product when they wear out. Stick with any product you like.

12 SKIN AND HAIR

Your skin is made up of layers of cells that cover your body and protect it from the environment. It also helps to get rid of excessive heat, a function of great importance during exercise.

Perspiration

Your temperature normally is about 98.6 degrees Fahrenheit because of all the activity going on inside it. The trillions of cells that make up your body are constantly working and using energy to keep you alive and active. All body processes generate heat, even when you are at rest. When you exercise, your metabolism speeds up, producing even more heat. Your muscles act like tiny furnaces, giving off heat as they convert and consume fuel. Exercise speeds up your heart, and your faster heart rate helps carry the warm blood from your muscles to your skin, where cooling can take place. When this greater volume of warm blood reaches your skin, the blood vessels in your skin widen, giving you a flushed appearance. Your skin perspires too. Evaporation of sweat helps to cool you off, keeping your temperature from rising too high. (See Chapter 4 for our discussion of hot weather.)

Body Odor

You've heard of underarm odor and foot odor, of course, but have you ever heard of forehead odor? No one else has heard of it either, since it doesn't exist. Not all sweat has the potential to smell bad. All

To Prevent Body Odor

1. Wash daily with antibacterial soap.
2. Use antiperspirants or deodorants.
3. Powder your skin.
4. Change clothes daily.
5. Wear socks.

sweat contains water and salt, neither of which causes odor. For sweat to produce an odor, it must contain significant amounts of fat and protein, too, which must be degraded by bacteria. Only the perspiration from your armpits, genitals, and breasts contain enough fat and protein to cause an odor when bacteria degrade them. The cells that your shoes and socks rub off from the skin on your feet remain in your shoes and socks, where bacteria can degrade them to produce an odor too. Skin elsewhere on your body produces sweat that is incapable of causing odor.

Sweat doesn't have any odor when it first appears on your skin. It takes about an hour for bacteria to make sweat smell. You can't avoid sweating when you exercise, and it would be dangerous to try to. Your body temperature can rise too high and make you pass out. However, there are several things you can do to prevent the sweat that causes body odor. Showering, particularly with an antibacterial soap, will wash away some of the bacteria that normally live on your skin. It will take several hours before more bacteria will appear on your skin. Deodorants contain zinc, aluminum, or zirconium, any of which help to kill bacteria. Antiperspirants contain the same metals in higher concentrations than in deodorants, thereby closing your sweat pores and preventing the sweat from coming out. They are not dangerous if you use them only in your armpits. Foot and body powders will absorb sweat, so that there will be less for bacteria to degrade. The odor you have depends on which kinds of bacteria live on your skin. Some cause body odor that smells like ammonia, while others cause body odor that smells like intestinal gas or feces. If your body odor is more unpleasant than you want it to be, try the techniques mentioned above to kill the bacteria or absorb the sweat.

Some people sweat so heavily in their armpits that water streams from their armpits to their hips. If this happens to you and makes you unhappy, check with your doctor, who can prescribe 20 percent aluminum chloride in alcohol. Apply this solution to your underarms before going to bed. Wrap Saran Wrap around your armpits after applying this solution, and leave this in place all night. If you feel any itching or burning, wash the solution off immediately, as it can cause a nasty burn in sensitive individuals. This procedure closes the pores leading from your sweat glands to your skin's surface. Your sweat won't be able to get to the surface for 7 to 10 days. When your armpits begin to sweat heavily again, repeat the procedure.

Oily Skin and Acne

Exercise doesn't affect acne at all. If you have acne, there's a lot that you can do to prevent and treat it, and you don't even have to think about curtailing your exercise.

Acne is due to a change in the consistency of the oil that is produced in your skin. To keep your skin from drying out, glands normally produce oil, which passes through pores to the surface of your skin. In acne, the colorless liquid oil is converted to a solid white material called sebum before the oil reaches the skin's surface.

A woman's body produces both masculinizing and feminizing hormones, which affect many parts of the body. Normal amounts of masculinizing hormones cause development of underarm and pubic hair, as well as oil production. Women who have excessive amounts of masculinizing hormones, such as testosterone, and women who are especially sensitive to normal amounts of these hormones can develop acne because these hormones enhance oil production and solidification.

If you have acne, your doctor should do some blood tests to determine if you have excessive amounts of these masculinizing hormones. For example, you should have blood tests to measure

---

The Treatment of Acne

Antibiotic lotions
Benzoyl peroxide topical preparations
Antibiotics by mouth
Certain types of birth control pills
Isotretinoin or large doses of Vitamin A
Drugs to block male hormones (spironolactone, cyproterone acetate)

your levels of dehydroepiandrosterone sulfate (DHEAS) and testosterone.

Bacteria in your skin also can cause the oil to harden. So, the treatment for acne is to reduce the bacterial content in your skin and to remove the solid oil plugs that have already formed. If your acne is severe, you may be treated with medication to lower your male hormone levels, even if your levels are normal.

If you have acne, you can buy a cream that contains 5 percent benzoyl peroxide at your drugstore. Once a day, apply it to the areas that have acne. If the cream irritates your skin, use it less frequently, such as every other day.

If the cream doesn't control your acne, check with a dermatologist. You will probably be given antibiotics. The simplest way to use antibiotics is to apply a solution of an antibiotic in alcohol to your face once or twice a day. Your dermatologist may also prescribe antibiotic pills, of which tetracycline is most commonly prescribed because it is the least expensive. If the antibiotic doesn't help you in six weeks, try another antibiotic. Taking it for a longer period of time won't make it more effective.

If the antibiotic regime doesn't work, you may need to take medication to lower the levels of your masculinizing hormones, or you may need to take large doses of Vitamin A (200,000 units of water-soluble Vitamin A daily) or a derivative of vitamin A, called 13-*cis* retinoic acid, or isotretinoin. This drug, which is sold under the brand name of Accutane, reduces oil production by your oil glands. It is a very effective drug, but it can also cause some serious side effects. It can damage your liver and raise your blood fat levels. So you must take blood tests every few weeks to see if anything is wrong. Because it can cause birth defects, a woman should not become pregnant while taking it.

As mentioned above, even if your hormone levels are normal, your acne may improve if you take hormones to lower your masculinizing hormone levels. Birth control pills can accomplish this, particularly those that are relatively estrogenic in balance. The most effective birth control pills for this purpose are Enovid, Ovulen, Demulen, and Ovcon. Other drugs that can lower masculinizing hormone levels and treat acne are spironolactone, cortisone-type pills, and cyproterone acetate. Discuss treatment with your doctor.

Dry Skin

Many people feel that they have to take a shower each time they exercise. Indeed, most people can shower, even twice a day, and suffer no ill effects at all. However, there are some people who have such dry, itchy skin that daily bathing would only make them itch and scratch.

Dry skin means lack of moisture, not lack of oil. However, you can't increase the amount of water in your skin by drinking more water. The water you drink doesn't lubricate your skin.

Almost 25 years ago, Dr. Harvey Blank of the University of Miami School of Medicine took a thick, dry callus and dipped it in oil. It remained hard as ever. He then took the same callus and dipped it in water. It became soft, but shortly after he took the callus out of the water, it dried out and became hard again. He then took the callus and dipped it in water. After it became soft, he dipped it in oil and it remained soft for hours.

This principle is basic to controlling dry skin: Soften your skin by bathing, then seal the moisture in your skin by covering it with oil immediately after you have bathed.

You don't have to shower or bathe every time you exercise, even though it is a lot more pleasant to do so. Most of us can avoid body odor after exercising by toweling off immediately after exercising, putting powder on our skin to help keep it dry, and wearing fresh clothes.

If you have dry skin and you feel that you must wash off each time after you exercise, you can help to protect your skin by doing the following:

- *Take showers rather than baths.* Staying in a bath for a long time strips away the covering of your skin, which helps to hold in moisture.
- *Use lukewarm rather than hot water.* Hot water removes more of the covering than lukewarm water.
- *Apply soap only to your armpits, genitals, feet, breasts, and face.* These are the only areas that produce sweat that can smell.
- *Apply creams immediately after showering.* The skin starts to lose moisture as soon as you get out of the shower. You have only a few minutes to seal the moisture in with creams.

Sun Exposure and Tanning Salons

Exercise certainly doesn't cause premature aging of the skin. However, those who exercise outdoors are exposed to the aging effects of sun exposure. With aging, the skin becomes thinner and its supporting tissue becomes weaker. Often fat is lost from underneath the skin at the same time. Wrinkling results, as youthful elasticity and firmness disappear. Sunlight accelerates this aging process. Forty-year-olds who continuously expose their bodies to sunlight develop leathery-looking skin that makes them appear much older.

Tanning salons are springing up all over the country. Some ads claim that the lamps emit ultraviolet A rays, which are safer than sunlight because they do not burn and do not cause cancer. These ads are wrong. There are two major types of light waves that cause the skin to tan: ultraviolet A rays and ultraviolet B rays. The UVB rays are more likely to cause skin cancer, while the UVA rays are more likely to cause aging of the skin.

It is true that UVA is less likely than UVB to cause burns and skin cancer. However, any ultraviolet ray, including UVA, can still cause burns and increase your chances of developing skin cancer.

Although dark-skinned people have a bit more natural protection against sun damage, all people are at risk of getting sunburns and skin damage from exposure to the same rays that offer a "healthy, sun-tanned look." Thus, tanning salons and sunbathing are dangerous to everyone, including those with dark skin color. Those who bask in the sun while young show premature aging of their skin as the years pass. Forty-year-old Jeannette and her 75-year-old mother look like 60-year-old sisters because Jeannette spent all of her summers at a swim club, while her mother avoided the sun throughout her life.

If your exercise keeps you outdoors, try to avoid sunlight as much as possible. Wear a sunscreen, a hat, and protective clothing. Avoid workouts between the hours of 10 A.M. and 2 P.M., when the sun is strongest. Your skin will remain younger-looking as a result.

If you insist on visiting tanning salons, make sure that you always wear goggles. Ultraviolet rays can damage your eyes too. It will be safer to start with a limited exposure to the rays and gradually increase the time that you spend under the lamps. However, we strongly recommend avoiding both tanning salons and outdoor sun exposure.

Athlete's Foot

Athlete's foot is a general term that can refer to several different kinds of dry, scaly, itchy conditions on your feet. Its most common cause is a fungus, but it may also stem from a bacterial infection, an allergy, or a skin disease, such as eczema. The different causes require different forms of treatment. All forms of athlete's foot can be painful and irritating, but all respond well to certain remedies. Your doctor can help pinpoint the cause and clear up the problem.

Any fungus is attracted to damp, dark places. So its most likely place to settle on you is in the spaces between your toes. Fungi are even more attracted to those spots where your skin gets rubbed a lot, such as the space between your fourth and fifth toes. If these areas are raw, irritated, dry, scaly, or cracked, you probably have a fungal infection, and it will probably respond well to the creams or pills your doctor prescribes.

If you have, between any of your toes, a rash that appears to stay very wet, you probably have a bacterial infection. Your doctor will scrape off some skin from between your toes and will culture it to detect any organisms. Such an infection can be treated with antibiotics.

A rash that is primarily on the top of your first two toes is most likely an allergy to one or more or the materials in your shoes or socks. If your doctor finds no evidence of an infection by the culture test, a piece of your shoe or sock will be taped to your back to detect an allergy to one of the materials inside. Such an allergy will cause a rash under the tape within a day or two. If you have an allergy, try getting new shoes, preferably a pair lacking the material to which you're allergic.

If your foot is red and scaly all over, but without a definite rash between your fourth and fifth toes, you probably have a foot eczema. This should be treated by keeping powder in your socks and changing your socks often, in order to keep your feet as dry as possible. A cortisone-like cream may help to hasten skin healing too.

Pseudomonas Folliculitis

If your skin begins to itch within a day or two after you have been in a whirlpool or hot tub, you probably have a skin infection called Pseudomonas folliculitis. This disease is caused by the bacteria Pseudomonas, and it is easily treated with carbenicillin pills. You can decrease your chances of getting this infection by showering immediately every time you emerge from a whirlpool or tub. If you notice such itching, check with your doctor, who will take a culture of your skin to confirm the cause of the infection. Although this infection isn't serious when it involves only your skin, it can progress, if untreated, to more serious infections that can spread throughout your body.

Blisters and Chafing

Blisters and chafing are caused by friction against your skin. Blisters usually occur in areas where your skin is very tight, such as your hands and feet. Chafing, on the other hand, affects parts of your body where the skin is looser and moves more freely, such as your inner thighs.

In areas where your skin is tight, the skin's bottom layer is fixed tightly in place and can't move with the top layer. So, when it's subjected to excessive rubbing, the top layer shears away from the bottom. The space created by the separation quickly fills with clear fluid from around your cells and bloodstream, and you have a *blister*. The skin is damaged and the fluid helps to cushion the area and prevent infection. Bowlers commonly get blisters on their thumbs, tennis players and golfers on their hands, and runners on their feet. Small-breasted women who run without a bra often get blisters around their nipples. Blisters are especially common on the feet because your blood pressure is highest there, and this high pressure usually fills these blisters with a lot of fluid.

Ill-fitting shoes are the most common cause of blisters, and the blister usually occurs where the rubbing is greatest. If your socks are too bulky and permit your feet to move around a lot inside your shoes, try wearing thinner socks or no socks at all. Better-fitting shoes will help too.

If you get a blister, be careful to keep the top layer of the skin in place. The blister will heal much faster and with much less pain. Removing the fluid will also help healing and relieve pain. Make a small hole at the edge of the blister with a sterilized needle. Press gently with your fingers to force out the fluid. Then apply an antiseptic ointment to prevent infection, and cover this with tape. If redness or pus develops around the blister, check with your doctor to see if you have an infection. If you do, you'll need an antibiotic to treat it.

Chafing is an abrasion of the outer layer of your skin. This happens when the skin is loose and can move as a single unit when it gets rubbed. Chafing can occur when your skin rubs against your clothes or against other skin. It's most common at the edge of your bra, at the seams of your shorts, or on the inner surfaces of your thighs, particularly if you are heavy. The best way to avoid chafing is by wearing shorts with soft seams or no seams between the legs, by wearing a bra that has soft edges and stays in place, and by keeping soft fabrics without seams between your thighs if your thighs must rub together (if they are bulky from either fat or muscle). *All* clothes for exercise should be made of soft fabrics with soft seams or no seams. Try powdering the areas that are particularly vulnerable before you work out. Wetness causes the skin to stick together, making it more likely to rub and cause friction. Powders absorb sweat and help to keep your skin dry. While moisture promotes chafing, heat promotes blisters, as occurs in the case of a bad sunburn. The combination of heat and moisture create the worst environment, making both blisters and chafing likely to occur.

The best way to prevent blisters and chafing is by reducing friction as much as possible and staying as dry as you can. Choose the right shoes and clothes. Use towels and other absorbent materials to dry off frequently. Use absorbent powders and lubricating jelly (such as petrolatum) in areas where rubbing is most likely to occur. You can place moleskin, a soft, adherent fabric, over irritating spots in your shoes to prevent them from rubbing against bony prominences in your feet.

Corns and Calluses

Calluses are areas of thickened skin without distinct borders that usually do not hurt. They are produced by your skin to give you extra padding and protection from repeated rubbing at bony prominences. Tennis players develop calluses on their palms from the pressure of their tennis racquets. Runners can get them on their soles just behind their toes from the pressure of their shoes.

Corns are painful lumps with distinct borders. They are caused by repeatedly rubbing the skin on your toes or palms. They have hard cores which dig into the skin to cause pain.

If calluses don't hurt, they do not need any treatment. If they do hurt, you can soak your feet in lukewarm water for a few minutes, rub bath oil on them, and then rub them with a pumice stone or emery board that you can buy at most drug stores.

If you can stop the rubbing that caused the calluses, they usually will go away with no other treatment. Hopefully, you can buy shoes that will not rub or you can go to a cobbler or podiatrist who will fit you for special inserts that can be placed in your shoes.

Corns usually are located over outgrowths of bone and they usually can be cured permanently only by having an orthopedist or podiatrist remove the prominent bone underneath. Temporary treatment is the same as for calluses.

TAKING CARE OF YOUR HAIR

When you exercise, sweat, salt, skin debris, and oil cling to your hair. These can make your hair dirty and your scalp itchy, leaving your hair dull-looking and limp. Shampooing refreshes your hair and scalp, making them feel a lot more comfortable.

Many women grew up with the mistaken notion that frequent shampooing is harmful. This myth is unfounded. There's nothing wrong with frequent shampooing, even as often as five times a day. Most of the shampoos on the market today are so mild that they will not damage your hair, regardless of how often you use them. Each hair shaft is covered with a protein layer called a cuticle, which is resistant to destruction by shampooing, even if frequent. The oil and dirt that are attached to the hair will be removed by the washing process, though, leaving your hair fresh and clean.

Don't be misled by some of the advertising claims about "pH-balanced shampoos," a term used to refer to shampoos that have been treated with acid to neutralize them. The cleaning agents in all shampoos are alkaline soaps and detergents. There is nothing wrong with alkaline shampoos. Adding acid does nothing to change the effects of the shampoo on your hair.

There is very little difference among the many shampoos available on the market today. Some smell nicer than others, but all do the job in the same way. Adding beer, herbs, vitamins, minerals, milk, eggs, or fragrances has no effect on the cleansing power of the shampoo either.

Many women avoid exercise because it takes so long to restore their hair after exercise. For them, washing is merely the beginning. If it takes more than a few minutes to fix your hair after you have washed it, you're probably wearing the wrong style. Long ago (and still for many women today, in fact), it was fashionable to have hair arranged in a rigid "hairdo," which required hair curlers to straighten or curl the hair and many hours of waiting for the finished product. The time and effort involved in the whole process made exercise virtually impossible.

Fortunately, styles and ideas about hair have changed a great deal. Hair is most manageable when it's cut to fall in its own natural way. Although many hairstylists don't know how to cut it to accomplish this, many others do. You must find one who specializes in cutting your hair to follow its natural lines, taking into account the direction of each hair shaft, the straightness or curliness of your hair, and the limited time in your busy day.

Conditioners are necessary only if your hair is long, dry, or thin, if it tangles when you try to comb it, or if you have a lot of split ends. Conditioners work by coating the hair shaft with a protective protein layer. If your conditioner is combined with your shampoo, it will get washed away as you rinse out the shampoo. The only effective way to use a conditioner is by applying it *after* you have already rinsed out the shampoo.

Although frequent shampooing won't damage your hair, harsh chemicals and instruments may. The hair is composed of three layers: an outer cuticle, a middle cortex, and an inner medulla. The outer cuticle is very tough and resistant to injury. It protects the weaker cortex and medulla.

Most of the pigment lies in the medulla. To change the color of your hair, dyes have to pass through the outer cuticle and get into the inner medulla. When they do this, they can damage the cuticle and weaken your hair. If you find that dyeing your hair causes it to break or fray, try using vegetable dyes. They are usually less potent than synthetic dyes and are less likely to damage your hair. If the vegetable dyes still damage your hair, you may have to keep your hair color.

Hair straighteners and permanent waves can also damage the outer cuticle, especially if they are used improperly or too frequently. If you tease your hair to create a bouffant look, you are combing the hair against its natural grain. This can damage the cuticle and break the hair. Vigorous brushing, braiding, or heating can also damage hair. The safest way to dry your hair is naturally, after blotting or rubbing gently with a towel to remove much of the water. If you prefer to blow-dry your hair for either speed or style, avoid close application of high temperatures. Use a cool or warm setting, rather than hot, or hold the dryer at least eight inches from your hair. Even hair sprays can cause trouble. Since they contain lacquer and alcohol to hold your hair in a rigid configuration, they can dry your hair excessively.

If you are unhappy about the appearance or manageability of your hair, consult a knowledgeable professional for advice. You should find out, before making any changes, whether the new look will work for you.

At various times of life, many women notice that their hair seems to be falling out in clumps. This is usually quite normal. All hairs normally go through a cycle of growing, resting, and then falling out. Since hairs do not have their cycles synchronized, hair loss is rarely obvious, even though as many as 100 hairs normally fall out every day. Certain hormones may lead to hair cycle synchronization, so that a lot more hairs than usual fall out at a time. For example, birth control pills and pregnancy can cause this, and sometimes the hair loss is greater after stopping birth control pills or after the end of pregnancy. Usually, such hair loss is only temporary and of no concern. However, if you seem to be losing a lot of hair, or if the loss continues for more than six months, consult a dermatologist.

13 SPECIAL MEDICAL PROBLEMS

Having read this far, you're now more intimately acquainted with your own body than 99 percent of your fellow humans are with theirs. This should be a source of some satisfaction to you as an intelligent, educated woman. Since you are so attuned to how your body works, you probably want to know even more about how exercise changes your body and how certain medical conditions affect your ability to exercise.

That's why we aren't through yet. This chapter is a semisystematized grab bag of facts, quirks, anomalies, conditions, and trivia associated with athletes and their bodies. A few of the subjects you've encountered before turn up here again because they deserve special mention and additional explanation. However, most of the information is new. It's designed to answer any questions you may have left and to finish the job of making you an expert on that most fascinating of topics, yourself.

THE CIRCULATORY SYSTEM

Your circulatory system, also called your cardiovascular system, consists of your heart and blood vessels. The blood vessels are divided into arteries, veins, and capillaries. Arteries carry blood from your heart throughout your body. Veins return the blood to your heart. Capillaries are tiny vessels where the exchange between arterial blood and venous blood takes place.

Athletic Veins and Varicose Veins

There is a big difference between enlarged athletic veins and enlarged varicose veins. Varicose veins are enlarged veins near the surface of the skin. They appear as wide blue lines, and they can be very painful. They're usually caused by malfunction of tiny valves inside your blood vessels. These valves are supposed to keep blood moving steadily in one direction, back toward your heart. When they aren't working right, gravity can cause blood to remain in your legs instead of moving toward your heart as it should. The blood remaining in your legs distends and enlarges the veins of your legs.

In athletes, veins are large because they're accustomed to carrying extra blood. Their width enables them to carry warm blood from your exercising muscles to your skin, where cooling can take place.

Exercise can help treat varicose veins. When you exercise your leg muscles, they help to pump blood back toward your heart, compensating for the valves' failure to do their job well. In contrast, sitting or standing still aggravates varicose veins. When you stand upright, you're encouraging the blood to collect in your legs because of gravity, and your muscles are not pumping to help circulate blood. Standing in high heels is worse yet. The unnatural elevation causes your muscles to remain contracted, so that they constrict the veins and create a further impediment to your circulation.

Support hose are of some benefit in alleviating varicose veins when you're standing fairly still. They produce some compression to help push the blood back toward your heart. You probably don't need them during exercise, though, since the force they exert is very small compared to the force exerted by your exercising muscles. Many women find them comfortable even for exercise. If you do, it's fine to wear them as long as you aren't exercising in a hot environment. They can interfere with your normal cooling mechanisms because they keep sweat from evaporating from the skin on your legs. If you wear them, you'll tire more quickly because your body will have to work harder to keep cool.

Rarely, clots can form in varicose veins. You can usually tell when this is happening to you. Such a vein will hurt to the touch, and may be red or swollen too. If this is the case, you shouldn't exercise. Vigorous movement could dislodge a clot, allowing it to travel through your bloodstream to one of your lungs, where it could endanger your life by obstructing the blood flow to this vital organ. Check with your doctor if your veins hurt.

Hemorrhoids

Hemorrhoids are painfully swollen varicose veins just inside or outside your rectum. They're caused by an obstruction to the flow of blood away from the area. Anything that blocks the blood flow, including benign or cancerous tumors, can cause hemorrhoids, but the most common causes are constipation and pregnancy.

A large muscle called the anal sphincter completely surrounds the opening to your rectum. It closes off the opening and prevents you from soiling yourself. In some people this sphincter can act like a tourniquet and compress all the blood vessels in the area, causing them to enlarge. The condition is rather common during pregnancy because the enlarged uterus presses down against the veins in your back, blocking blood flow in these veins, which enlarge as a result.

Exercise helps to prevent hemorrhoids by improving circulation and preventing constipation. Other techniques for avoiding constipation will help too, such as drinking a lot of fluids, eating a high-fiber diet, and avoiding highly refined starches (like white bread and spaghetti). If you already have hemorrhoids, you can reduce your discomfort by using soft, wet instead of rough, dry toilet paper, or by using a bidet. Soothing ointments or petroleum jelly may reduce irritation in this sensitive area. Injections of cortisonelike medication may offer temporary relief, as may ointments containing cortisonelike drugs. The most successful treatment for hemorrhoids is to stretch the anal sphincter and tear some of its fibers. This reduces the pressure on the blood vessels. This procedure leads to no change in bowel function. Other methods of treating hemorrhoids include tying them off and cutting them out. If your hemorrhoids don't bother you, leave them alone. If they are causing you discomfort, discuss them with your doctor.

Athlete's Heart

Sometimes, athletes with strong healthy hearts can be misdiagnosed as having sick hearts. Both strong and weak hearts may have similar electrocardiogram abnormalities and slow pulse rates.

Your heart is divided into four chambers: two atria and two ventricles. The major pumping chamber is called the left ventricle. Both athletes and people in heart failure have enlarged left ventricles, a fact that can cause considerable confusion.

In the athlete, the thickening is the result of large, strong, efficient muscle fibers, conditioned by pushing out a great volume of blood. A diseased heart, on the other hand, has a left ventricle enlarged because its small, weak muscle is stretched like a balloon.

An electrocardiogram may not be sensitive enough to measure the difference between a healthy muscular heart and a sick weak heart. An electrocardiogram measures only the electricity that is produced in the heart. Each beat starts when an electric current originates in the upper part of the heart. As the electric current passes down the heart, the heart muscle contracts. Having a weak heart does not necessarily change the electrical activity of the heart. Having a strong muscular heart does not necessarily change the electricity either.

A slow pulse rate can mean that you have a healthy or a diseased heart. An athlete has a slow heart rate because her heart muscle can pump more blood with each contraction and, thus, doesn't need to pump as often to deliver a given amount of blood. A slow heart rate in an athlete is usually a sign of fitness. However, a sick heart may also beat slowly. Some of the electric currents that start each beat in the upper part of the heart may not be able to get through to the rest of the heart because the nerves that carry the current are damaged. Then the heart will not beat as often.

For these reasons, athletes are sometimes misdiagnosed as having abnormal or diseased hearts. Further testing is needed in these cases, preferably by a doctor familiar with the way a very healthy heart can mimic the symptoms of a very sick one.

Athletic "Anemia"

Regular exercise probably won't make you anemic, but it may make you appear so. The confusion lies with the way the red blood cell concentrations are measured. Anemia is a disease characterized by an abnormally-low red blood cell count. This means you have too few red blood cells altogether. The number of red cells in your blood is approximated by measuring the number in a small sample, and this is expressed as a concentration. Blood concentrations are figured as the ratio of the cells in question to total blood volume. Regular exercise causes your blood volume to increase by as much as 10 percent, while the number of your red blood cells are increasing much less. Raising the volume much more than the cell count leads to dilution of the red blood cells. This means that the red cells have a lower concentration. Technically, this is anemia, but actually it is not. The total number of red cells in your bloodstream is normal in this "dilutional anemia."

Some athletes also have a real anemia, though, possibly because they consume too little iron in their diets, and possibly because they lose iron through their intestines during heavy training. Some athletes in heavy training lose increased amounts of blood in their stools. The mechanism of this blood loss is not known. It is possible that vigorous exercise diverts blood from the intestines to the exercising muscles. If this happens, the lack of blood flow to the intestines may damage the intestinal linings, allowing blood to leak into the stool.

If you have a real anemia that is due to iron deficiency, an integral part of your treatment will be taking supplements of iron, the mineral necessary for the manufacture of red cells. Even if you haven't developed anemia, you may have deficient iron stores—25 percent of all women of reproductive age do. Less than 50 percent of the iron in your body is in your red blood cells. Most of the iron is stored in your liver, spleen, bone marrow, and other tissues. You must deplete almost all of the iron stored in your bones and liver before you develop anemia (that is, before the concentration of red blood cells drops abnormally low). Anemia can impair an athlete's performance, and iron deficiency can too.

You can determine the approximate amount of your iron stores by having a blood test called a *ferritin* level, which will be low if you are iron-deficient. If you have a low concentration of red cells in your blood, you are anemic. To confirm that your anemia is due to iron-deficiency, your blood can be smeared on a slide and examined under a microscope. If your red cells appear small and pale, you probably have iron-deficiency anemia. (You could also have thalassemia, a hereditary anemia.) If you are iron-deficient, you should take iron supplements. Most people who eat meat, fish or chicken daily get enough iron in their diets. If you don't eat these foods every day, you are more likely to be iron-deficient. Women who menstruate lose some iron in each period and often need extra iron to replace this loss. Many women who menstruate will benefit from taking two or three iron tablets each week (each containing about 100 milligrams of ferrous sulfate). It is unlikely that any woman who menstruates will be harmed by doing this. Excessive iron consumed usually passes out from your body in your stools. Your stools will turn dark black when they contain a lot of iron.

Blood Pressure

Blood pressure is the force that your blood exerts on your blood vessels as it circulates through your body. It is measured as the force needed to raise a column of mercury one millimeter. Your blood pressure has two components: the systolic pressure, which is the pressure in your blood vessels when your heart muscle contracts, and the diastolic pressure, which is the pressure in your blood vessels when your heart muscle relaxes. If these numbers in your case are 120 and 80, respectively, your blood pressure would be expressed as 120/80 millimeters of mercury, which is perfectly normal blood pressure.

High blood pressure is defined as a resting systolic pressure above 135 or a resting diastolic pressure above 85. It is normal for your blood pressure to be higher during and after exercise or emotional stress. Often it can rise even from the stress of visiting your doctor's office. Having high blood pressure at rest can increase your chances of having a heart attack, stroke, and kidney failure. It should always be treated in order to avoid these problems.

About 20 percent of adult Americans have high blood pressure, although most of them have no symptoms. Because this condition produces symptoms so rarely until serious damage has been done, the only way to tell that your blood pressure is high is by having it measured. Ask your doctor to check your blood pressure at least once every year. If your pressure is very high, you should be taking medication to lower it. If your pressure is only mildly elevated, you may be able to reduce it by exercising, avoiding stimulants (cigarettes, coffee, tea, chocolate, and cola drinks), decreasing your salt intake, and losing weight if you're overweight. Most people would benefit from reducing the salt in their diets. (See Chapter 2 for a thorough discussion of your salt needs.)

During aerobic exercise (such as jogging, dancing, swimming, or cycling), your heart rate rises, your systolic blood pressure rises, and your diastolic pressure remains the same or rises slightly. These effects are caused mostly by the stimulating chemicals, such as adrenaline and noradrenaline, produced by your sympathetic nervous system. Aerobic exercise activates your sympathetic nervous system much less if you are training regularly, so that your blood vessels will be more relaxed and will impose less resistance against blood flow. As a result, your blood pressure at rest will be lower, and the changes in your heart rate and blood pressure during exercise will be much smaller when you are conditioned.

During static exercise (such as weight lifting or isometric exercises), your heart rate, systolic blood pressure, and diastolic blood pressure all increase. This type of exercise may be dangerous for people with heart disease because the increased pressure could cause a damaged heart to beat irregularly or could burst a blood vessel anywhere in your body. If your blood pressure falls during exercise, your heart is probably too weak to pump blood through your body in response to the increased demands imposed by exercise. If you feel dizzy or weak or if you faint during exercise, you should stop exercising immediately. You may have heart disease, and you should see a doctor to find out what's wrong.

Cold Showers

Many people find cold showers invigorating, and for most people they're perfectly safe. However, people with high blood pressure or certain forms of heart disease should avoid them.

Do you remember what happens when your internal body temperature rises? The blood vessels in your skin widen to help dissipate the excess heat. The opposite happens when your body temperature falls. Cold temperatures constrict the blood vessels in your skin, so that more blood remains internally, keeping your vital organs warm. Whenever the blood vessels in your skin narrow, your blood pressure rises. This can be dangerous for people with heart disease. Cold temperatures or the higher blood pressures they cause can lead to irregular heartbeats too, another danger for damaged hearts.

Orthostatic Hypotension

Orthostatic hypotension is low blood pressure as you stand up. This condition, which is usually harmless, can make you feel dizzy and weak, particularly when you stand up quickly. Surprisingly, being in good physical condition can make you more susceptible to this problem.

As you know, the better the shape you're in, the slower your heart beats. This is because training strengthens your heart, so that it can pump more blood with each beat. As a result, it doesn't have to beat as often to supply your body with blood. Athletes frequently have heart rates less than 60 beats a minute.

When you rise from lying to sitting or from sitting to standing, gravity reduces the blood in your head briefly. It can take several seconds for your slow-beating, healthy heart to pump enough blood to your head to eliminate the light-headed feeling you had during the temporary fall in blood pressure in your head. If standing up makes you feel dizzy and weak or makes you see black spots before your eyes, get into the habit of rising more slowly.

Dehydration can aggravate orthostatic hypotension by reducing your blood volume. So you are more likely to have this problem after hot-weather workouts. Be sure to drink plenty of fluids.

If rising slowly and drinking fluids don't prevent these symptoms, check with your doctor. Orthostatic hypotension can signal unhealthy conditions too, such as heart disease or anemia.

THE RESPIRATORY SYSTEM

Your respiratory system governs your breathing. Your main organs of respiration are, of course, your lungs. To the extent that they figure in breathing, your nose and mouth are also part of this system. So is your windpipe, or trachea.

Exercise-Induced Asthma

While running with her classmates, Jody suddenly started gasping for breath and dropped off the pace. Her coach accused her of being a quitter. She wasn't. She had exercise-induced asthma. Fortunately, a correct diagnosis and good treatment prevented her from losing all interest in sports, and today she can compete successfully in any game she chooses. Not all asthma victims are so lucky.

Asthma is the intermittent obstruction of the tubes that carry air to and from your lungs. In some people, the condition is brought on *only* by exercise. Breathing hard and fast causes water to evaporate rapidly from the tubes leading to the lungs, and this causes the tubal linings to cool. As a result, the tubes constrict and fill up with mucus.

Several million Americans suffer from exercise-induced asthma, and it's very common among children. A person subject to it may be able to exercise very well for 8 to 12 minutes. Then she may start to cough and become short of breath. Her symptoms may continue for several minutes to an hour after she stops exercising. The condition is far more severe in the winter, when the air is cold and dry. Of all athletes, swimmers are least susceptible to exercise-induced asthma because they breathe warm, moist air. Runners are most susceptible to it, particularly in the winter, since they breathe cold, dry air.

Women whose bronchial tubes react to rapid breathing of cold, dry air by constricting will not experience any wheezing when they exercise in a closed bathroom with hot water running at full speed from the shower. Breathing warm, moist air reduces the likelihood of having an asthma attack. On particularly cold days, you can warm and moisten the air you're breathing by wrapping a woolen scarf around your head in such a way that your mouth is covered but your eyes are exposed.

If you're very strong and very well conditioned, you may find it possible to "run through" an asthma attack; that is, you may be able to keep working out while the tubes clear gradually on their own. But you should never try this unless you're in absolutely top shape and have medical assistance nearby. You may become so short of breath that you need an injection of adrenaline to open your breathing tubes.

Careful training can delay the onset of asthma attacks and can teach people to handle their attacks too. Consult a doctor, preferably an internist or allergist, if you have asthma. Together, you can develop an exercise program specifically for you. You may need medication too, such as salbutamol or cromolyn, both of which are safe drugs that can be inhaled immediately before you exercise.

Hyperventilation

In the excitement before a sports competition, have you ever found yourself suddenly immobilized with frozen muscles, labored breathing, nausea, dizziness, a headache, or an eerie tingling in your toes or lips? If so, you were probably hyperventilating (breathing too fast). Hyperventilation eliminates carbon dioxide from your bloodstream rapidly, making your blood more alkaline and, in turn, imbalancing several minerals in your body. All the symptoms listed above can result.

This syndrome is very common among children, particularly among those who react very emotionally to the challenge of competition. Some people, both adults and children, mistakenly believe that hyperventilating can fill their lungs with more oxygen, so that they can perform better or longer. Since the blood coming from your lungs is normally 99 percent saturated with oxygen, breathing faster won't fill them more. Your body is geared to regulate its own breathing, depending on how much oxygen it needs. This happens automatically, without any voluntary actions on your part. Exercise naturally increases your breathing rate as you need more oxygen to meet the needs of your exercising muscles. If you force yourself to breathe faster than your body is breathing naturally, either before or while exercising, you'll increase your chances of developing the unpleasant symptoms listed above.

Fortunately, hyperventilation is easy to treat. Put a paper bag over your head. This will force you to inhale the air you've just exhaled, containing the carbon dioxide. This will restore the normal pH balance to your blood, and the symptoms should disappear promptly.

Since the rapid, labored breathing of hyperventilation can mimic that of asthma, sometimes it is difficult to distinguish between these conditions. However, an asthma victim wheezes and cannot get enough air, while a victim of hyperventilation has no wheezing and is getting too much air.

Coughing

Coughing a lot when you work out usually presents no problem beyond the annoying symptom itself. The cough probably results from producing more mucus to help you reduce irritation from pollutants in the air you're breathing. This cough is nothing to worry about.

Nasal Breathing

Your nose does a wonderful job of warming and filtering the air you inhale, but your nostrils aren't large enough to transmit enough air during exercise. Even though your mouth isn't as efficient for heating and filtering air, its cross-sectional area is 10 times larger than that of your nose. So it's capable of moving much more air into and out of your lungs. Don't worry about the dirt and pollutants that can get through. Your respiratory tract contains hairlike cilia and mucus which prevent the undesirable particles from reaching your lungs. During exercise, you can't inhale and exhale enough air through your nose. You *should* breathe through your mouth.

Nosebleeds

If your nose is already irritated—possibly by a cold or by breathing cold, dry air—heavy breathing caused by exercise may irritate it more and may bring on a nosebleed. If you get one, don't follow the conventional advice of lying down or tilting your head backward. This will only make you swallow the blood, an action that can nauseate you. Instead, sit upright and press on both sides of your nose, using your thumb and index finger to grip the soft flesh underneath the cartilage. Since more than 75 percent of all nosebleeds originate in the blood vessels you'll be compressing, a clot should form and the bleeding probably will stop within about 10 minutes. If this trick doesn't work, contact your doctor. The blood may be coming from elsewhere and you may need professional help to stop it.

If your nose starts to bleed after you've bumped it, check quickly to see if it appears to be broken. Look in a mirror to determine if your nose is crooked, and gently feel with your fingers to see if it moves more freely than it used to. If you have either of these signs of a fracture, see a doctor as soon as possible. A broken nose usually becomes so swollen within a few hours of the accident that surgical correction of the damage becomes much more difficult.

Earaches

Hard breathing during exercise, particularly in cold weather, can cause earaches and temporary deafness. Although no permanent damage is likely to result, these symptoms can be very unpleasant.

Each of your ears is connected to the back of your throat by a tube called a eustachian tube. Normally, cells lining your middle ear produce fluid that flows down this tube into your throat, where you unconsciously swallow the fluid along with your saliva. Rapid breathing during exercise in cold air can irritate the lining of your throat, which can swell, blocking the eustachian tubes. When this happens, the middle-ear fluid has nowhere to go. So it builds up in your ear, causing pressure and pain.

Fluid accumulation in your ear can impair your hearing by muffling vibrations. When sound waves normally reach your eardrum, a tightly stretched membrane, they vibrate a small bone attached to the eardrum. This bone transmits a nerve impulse to your brain, which interprets the message as sound. Any accumulation of fluid in your ear can prevent proper vibrations on the bone, and this can impair your hearing or produce strange sounds in your ears.

Often, you can avoid this problem by wrapping a woolen scarf loosely around your face, so that it covers your mouth but not your ears. This allows you to breathe warm, moist air. If this doesn't work, you may be better off running in place inside on very cold days.

A Word About Second Wind

Second wind is a myth. It doesn't exist. During a hard workout, you may reach a point where you're severely short of breath. Then, suddenly, you seem to recover. You feel revived and breathe much more easily. When people refer to second wind, they are talking about this recovery from the oxygen debt incurred during heavy exertion. It isn't the miracle it seems to be, though. What really happens is that you slow down enough to repay your body's oxygen debt.

As we discussed in Chapter 1, your need for oxygen increases when you exercise. You breathe harder to keep up with the heightened demand. When you exceed your anaerobic threshold, you develop an oxygen debt, since you aren't inhaling enough oxygen to meet your needs. If you slow the pace of your workout (often subconsciously), your oxygen intake will catch up with your decreasing demand, and you will repay the debt. When balance is restored, you will feel much better and can accelerate your pace again. Your body arranges its own, natural recovery.

THE GASTROINTESTINAL SYSTEM

Your gastrointestinal system, also called your digestive system, is responsible for processing the food you eat. It converts food into sugar and fatty acids that your body can use for fuel, as described in Chapter 2, and it eliminates waste products. This marvel of organic plumbing includes all the tubing that runs from your mouth to your rectum, notably your stomach and small and large intestine. Your liver and pancreas also belong to this system.

Athletic "Liver Disease"

Certain abnormal blood tests that are common among athletes can mimic liver disease. This happens because the same enzymes are released by damaged liver cells and by fatigued muscle cells. If your blood has high concentrations of the enzymes SGOT (serum glutamic oxalacetic transaminase), SGPT (serum glutamic pyruvic transaminase), LDH (lactic dehydrogenase), and CPK (creatine phospho-kinase), stop training for 48 hours and see if the levels return to normal. If they do, your liver is probably fine. (Enzyme levels elevated by exercise always return to normal within 48 hours.) If the values remain elevated, ask your doctor for a thorough evaluation.

Exercising after Eating

When you exercise, less blood flows to your stomach, and food already in your stomach will probably remain there. Most women find it uncomfortable to feel food sloshing around during vigorous exercise. If you do, avoid eating for at least two hours before you exercise. Since liquids usually pass through your stomach within 30 minutes, the waiting period after a liquid meal doesn't have to be quite as long as after a solid meal. Despite the old wives' tale to the contrary, you are very unlikely to develop stomach cramps and drown from swimming after eating. However, you may prefer to avoid the uncomfortable feeling anyway. If you can exercise comfortably immediately after eating, there is no medical reason to avoid it. Your body will tell you what it prefers, and most athletes prefer to listen to this particular signal.

Diabetes

Diabetics need to exercise. Read on and you'll see why. Diabetes is caused by a lack of insulin from your pancreas or an inability of your body to respond to insulin. Diabetics have high blood sugar levels. This causes sugar to attach to certain tissues, such as arteries and nerves, and damage them.

When your blood sugar level reaches a certain concentration, your pancreas releases insulin, which causes sugar to leave the bloodstream and enter certain cells. Most cases of diabetes that start after the age of 40 are due to inability of the body to respond adequately to insulin, rather than to a lack of insulin.

Insulin Receptors

Consider the cells in your body as balloons full of fluid. On the surface of the cells are binding sites for insulin called insulin receptors. Insulin must first attach to the insulin receptor before it can do its job of pushing sugar into the cell. If there are not enough insulin receptors, the insulin finds it difficult to attach to the receptors and

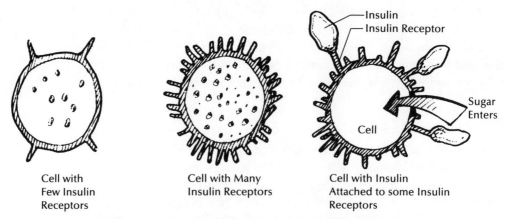

Cell with
Few Insulin
Receptors

Cell with Many
Insulin Receptors

Cell with Insulin
Attached to some Insulin
Receptors

Figure 13-1. How Insulin Permits Sugar to Enter Cell.

more insulin is required to do the job. Anything that increases the number of insulin receptors makes insulin more efficient. Anything that decreases insulin receptors makes diabetes worse.

Exercise helps most diabetics to require less insulin. It increases the number of insulin receptors by a yet-unknown mechanism. Eating high-carbohydrate foods, such as bread, pasta, vegetables, and beans, does the same. Eating fat and being fat decrease the number of insulin receptors.

If you are a juvenile-onset diabetic, you'll have to schedule your exercise, meals, and insulin carefully and in advance. If you take in too much insulin before you exercise, you can develop low blood sugar, which will make you tired and can even cause you to pass out.

Ketones

Your body uses fat and sugar for energy. Ketones are breakdown products formed when your body uses fat for energy. Your body then can use the ketones for energy also. As long as your body can use sugar for energy, in addition to fat, it can break down the ketones so that they will not accumulate in your bloodstream. However, when your body cannot use sugar for energy, it must use fat almost exclusively. Then fat is broken down so rapidly that many ketones are formed. Your body cannot break down the ketones and they accumulate in your bloodstream. When ketones accumulate in your bloodstream, it is a signal that your body is burning large amounts of fat. The ketones by themselves are not harmful.

If diabetics do not take enough insulin before exercising, their bodies may not be able to get sugar inside certain cells that need it for energy. When this happens, these cells must burn large amounts of fat for energy. The fats will be broken down into ketones, which can accumulate in their bloodstreams. The ketones make their muscles and blood more acidic. This tires them, makes their muscles hurt, and can even make them feel sick.

In spite of this, it is better for a diabetic to take in too little insulin rather than too much before exercising. During exercise, your muscles can use sugar without needing insulin. The brain never needs insulin to use sugar. So, it is possible for a diabetic to exercise, even though she has not taken an adequate dose of insulin.

On the other hand, if the diabetic takes too much insulin, she can develop a low blood sugar level, which will make her tired and can even cause her to pass out.

If a diabetic has a high blood level of ketones before she starts to exercise, her body does not have enough insulin and, as a result, will burn mostly fat. The ketone level will rise further during exercise and she will tire earlier.

To check for ketone levels, a diabetic can buy special paper strips at any drug store. The strips are dipped into her urine. If ketones are present in her blood, they will also be in her urine, and the sticks will turn purple within a few seconds.

Practical Considerations

If you are a diabetic you should eat a meal three to five hours before you exercise or compete and you should take your insulin at its regular time. The insulin should not be injected over the muscles that will be heavily exercised, as the insulin may be absorbed too rapidly and cause the blood sugar level to drop too low. For example, before a competition, a runner should inject insulin in her abdomen or back. During exercise, food should be available to treat low blood sugar. Heavily sugared drinks can be used during exercise, since the muscles will draw the sugar rapidly from the bloodstream and the blood sugar level will not rise significantly.

Flatulence

Intestinal gas is usually caused by the failure of your body to process certain carbohydrates. As discussed in Chapter 2, all carbohydrates are made up of sugars alone or bound together. Since only single sugars can be absorbed through your intestines into your bloodstream, all carbohydrates larger than single sugars must be degraded in your intestines by specific enzymes. Those that are degraded are absorbed, and those that are not degraded pass into your large intestine, where bacteria ferment them, releasing gas (most commonly hydrogen and carbon dioxide) in the process.

Theoretically, you should be able to break down all the carbohydrates you eat into single sugars. However, this doesn't happen in all cases. Sometimes the carbohydrate is too complex to be degraded easily, as occurs with the starch in most beans. If you soak beans in water for at least three hours or boil them for at least 30 minutes, much of the carbohydrate is broken down so that it can be absorbed, and it is far less likely to cause gas.

Some people lack the necessary enzyme to accomplish the degradation, as happens to many people who can't drink milk comfortably. Such people have inadequate amounts of the enzyme lactase, which is needed to break down the milk sugar lactose. When they consume large amounts of any dairy product, the lactose passes into their large intestines, where bacteria ferment it, forming gas and causing diarrhea too.

Gas can be more than just a social embarrassment. If it's not released, it can stretch your lower bowel enough to cause painful cramps. If this is a problem for you, you may want to try eliminating from your diet the foods that commonly cause gas: first milk and other dairy products, then all bread and other products made from wheat, rye, and barley. If you still have a problem, discuss your diet with a nutritionist or doctor.

Many people who are not bothered by gas most of the time become quite flatulent when they exercise. This is because exercise hastens intestinal motility, speeding the passage of food through

---

FOODS MOST LIKELY TO CAUSE INTESTINAL GAS

Milk	Brussels sprouts	Potatoes
Onions	Wheat germ	Eggplant
Dried Beans	Bagels	Citrus fruits
Celery	Pretzels	Apples
Carrots	Prunes	Bread
Raisins	Apricots	
Bananas	Pastries	

your intestines and exaggerating the production of gas too. Since food moves through an athlete's intestines more rapidly than through a sedentary person's, it has less time to be processed properly in the small intestine, and more of it may end up as gas. As a result, it's very common to pass gas when you exercise, particularly if your diet contains a lot of foods that produce gas. If this gas bothers you or those with whom you exercise, try to reduce your consumption of the foods most likely to produce gas.

Diarrhea

Diarrhea, the explosive expulsion of loose, watery stools, is never normal. It's a disease state usually caused by virus, bacteria, or parasites. However, it also occurs in some athletes who get dehydrated and then compensate by drinking large amounts of fluids very fast. As discussed above, athletes who lack certain intestinal enzymes get gas and diarrhea when they eat carbohydrates they can't degrade. Although people can develop diarrhea while they are not exercising, they are even more likely to develop diarrhea when they exercise. Physical activity aggravates the problem by accelerating the passage of foods through your intestines, allowing less time for proper processing. If you have this problem, eliminate the culprits from your diet altogether or avoid eating them within six hours before exercise.

Bloody Stools

Bright red blood in your stools is probably caused by hemorrhoids, or fissures (small cracks in the opening to the rectum). Internal bleeding from the lining of your stomach or intestines (from an ulcer or growth) usually causes a tarry discoloration of your stools, as the bright red blood is mixed with intestinal contents to form a tarry color. The tarry appearance of blood in your stool is usually very different from the black discoloration caused by iron supplementation. Bloody stools are always abnormal and should always be checked by a doctor.

Constipation

This is a condition in which bowel movements are extremely infrequent and difficult. Since exercise hastens the passage of food through the intestines, this problem is very rare among women who exercise regularly.

Many women mistakenly believe that they must have a bowel movement every day. This is not so. If you eat a low fiber diet, relatively little waste will accumulate and your bowel movements may be less frequent and smaller. This can be quite normal. However, if your bowel movements are very hard and are painful to pass, several remedies may be helpful.

- Limit your intake of refined starches, such as white bread.
- Eat more high fiber foods, such as whole grains (especially bran), raw fruits, and vegetables.
- Drink plenty of fluids.
- Exercise regularly, particularly in aerobic sports.

Most adults require 24 hours to pass an entire meal through their intestines. Some marathoners can process the same meal in six hours.

THE URINARY SYSTEM

The urinary system includes your kidneys and your bladder. Stress urinary incontinence is the most common problem among exercising women and was thoroughly discussed in Chapter 10.

Bloody Urine

Although this has been noticed among joggers and has even been referred to as "jogger's kidney," this problem is usually associated with exercises much more strenuous than jogging. Bloody urine is more common among men than among women. The blood can leak from the wall of the bladder as it bangs against the bones and organs that surround it. Exercise also shakes up the kidneys so that they may also leak blood.

Blood is obvious when it colors your urine red or maroon, but it can be present even when your urine appears clear and colorless. Such blood must be detected by a microscopic examination of your urine, a test that should be done if you have had obvious (red) blood in your urine that now seems to have resolved. Exercise-induced bleeding from the bladder or kidney is usually harmless and should always resolve within 48 hours without exercising. If you have blood in your urine after exercising, avoid exercise for 48 hours and then have a microscopic urine examination performed by your doctor or a laboratory. If you still have red blood cells present in your urine, check with your doctor for a more thorough evaluation to find the cause of the problem. You may have an infection or an abnormality in your kidney or bladder and may need medication or surgery to correct the problem.

THE IMMUNE SYSTEM

This is the system that allows you to fight off infections. A healthy immune system is on the alert to identify, capture, and destroy invading organisms foreign to your body. There is no convincing evidence that exercise affects your immunity, unless you're overtraining. One of the early signs of training too much is an increased susceptibility to developing colds.

Exercising When You're Sick

Although we certainly recommend exercising when you're healthy, we believe that it's probably safer to take a few days off during most illnesses. If you are a competitive athlete and develop a cold when you have an important competitive event in the next few weeks, you can continue to train, but only if you do not have a fever and if your muscles do not hurt when you exercise. If you continue to train, you should do so at a decreased level. Colds always take away some of your strength and endurance.

Most colds are caused by viruses, and there is no evidence that mild exercise will make your cold symptoms worse or that it will prolong the time it takes for you to recover. In fact, complete bedrest won't even help you to recover faster. Military recruits who were put to bed at the first sign of any infection did not heal faster than those who were kept in basic training.

During exercise, your body produces large amounts of heat. Your heart not only must pump blood to your muscles to supply them with oxygen, but also must pump large amounts of blood from your hot muscles to your skin where the heat can be dissipated.

If you have a fever when you start to exercise, your temperature will rise even higher during exercise and your heart must work even harder to keep your temperature from rising too high. Occasionally with colds, your heart muscle can be affected and you can develop irregular heartbeats during exercise.

Some viruses infect your muscles and cause them to hurt. Exercising when your muscles hurt increases their chances of being torn. So, there are several reasons to postpone exercising during viral infections, such as colds, though most people can exercise moderately anyway without suffering any ill effect.

COMING BACK AFTER AN OPERATION

After any surgery, you'll be anxious to resume training as soon as possible. How soon you can safely resume your old habits will depend on the type of operation you've had and how soon you can exercise without pain. Your own comfort will be your best guide. Pain usually indicates that healing is incomplete, and you should never exercise if it causes pain to do so. Different operations require different recovery times, but the rule of listening to your body still applies.

Any abdominal operation will leave your belly sore. Examples of abdominal operations include appendectomy (removal of your appendix,), cholecystectomy (removal of your gall bladder), abdominal hysterectomy (removal of your uterus through an incision in your abdomen), and tubal ligation (tying your Fallopian tubes). The healing process begins as soon as the operation has ended, and it takes at least 10 days to form a strong scar. How soon you can exercise after such an operation depends on the strength of your healing incision (through the skin and all deeper layers) and the abdominal forces incurred during the exercise. No scientific studies have been done to assess how soon you can safely resume exercising after an abdominal operation. However, pain generally decreases as healing progresses and can serve as a fairly reliable guide for safe activity. If it hurts to exercise, postpone your planned sport until you can do it painlessly. It takes most people at least a month to be able to exercise at all, and it often takes as long as nine months to be able to resume your previous level comfortably.

After a vaginal operation that involves the inside of your abdomen (such as a vaginal hysterectomy), similar healing must take place. Since your abdominal skin hasn't been cut, your abdominal muscles haven't been stretched or cut, and the fibrous sheath surrounding these muscles hasn't been cut either, you'll probably encounter less pain after a vaginal operation (compared to what you would have experienced after an abdominal operation). You'll probably be able to resume exercising sooner as a result. To reduce your risk of infection, though, you should avoid swimming and other water sports for at least three weeks after a vaginal hysterectomy, and you should avoid putting anything into your vagina for that time also.

After a minor vaginal operation, such as a dilatation and curettage (D&C), you can probably resume exercising the same day or the next day. Of course, if the D&C was performed because you had been bleeding heavily for a long time, you may have lost so much blood before the operation that you may be iron-deficient or anemic. Either of these conditions can make you tire sooner and can impair your athletic performance. However, there is no medical reason to avoid exercising after a D&C, regardless of the reason for which it was done (for example, termination of pregnancy, miscarriage, or abnormal bleeding). The only exceptions to this are swimming and other water sports. You should avoid all water sports for at least two weeks after a D&C and should avoid putting anything into your vagina during that time also.

Recovery will probably take longer after an orthopedic or podiatric operation on one of your legs or feet than after an abdominal or vaginal operation. The specific operation will dictate how soon you can resume any exercise. The great stresses running and cycling impose on the bones, muscles, and joints of your legs will probably make it advisable to postpone these sports longer, in order to permit optimal healing. Surgery on bones usually requires a minimum of eight weeks for healing and often considerably longer.

Back surgery usually requires months to a year for recovery, too, depending on the specific procedure that has been done.

Surgery on your upper body rarely requires much delay in resuming running, unless the arm and upper-body motions of running cause pain. However, you should postpone swimming and rowing longer after procedures on your upper body. Minor procedures on parts of your body that are not used for your sport usually permit resumption of your sport on the day of the procedure, although running often causes pain by shaking the incisions involved.

You should probably wait at least a week before resuming running, jumping, stretching, or lifting weights after cosmetic surgery, in order to permit the scar to heal as imperceptibly as possible. Your plastic surgeon may suggest a longer delay, and you should follow any such advice, of course.

How soon you can resume exercising after an operation is rarely affected by the level of fitness you had before. However, the stronger most of your muscles are, the more easily you can take care of yourself without using the muscles that hurt. For example, people with weak arm muscles use their abdominal and leg muscles to help them close heavy automobile doors. So it may hurt to close your car door after an abdominal operation if you need your abdominal muscles to help your arms. If your arms were strong enough to close the door without assistance, you'll be able to do this comfortably after such an operation. This principle applies to other muscle groups and other operations too. Most people don't get much advance notice before scheduling necessary operations. So it's a good idea to strengthen all of your muscles now and to maintain this strength, in case you need an operation someday.

Your surgeon is responsible for the outcome of your operation and how you recover from it. Therefore, you should always follow his or her advice. Be sure to tell your doctor before the operation how important exercise is to you. This information may modify the recommendations you are given.

If you can't exercise in a particular sport for a while, you may be able to maintain your cardiovascular fitness in another sport. This will enable you to regain your former pace and endurance sooner once you can return to your sport. Check with your doctor to be sure.

THE MUSCULOSKELETAL SYSTEM

This includes your bones, muscles, joints, cartilage, tendons, and ligaments. Most important topics on this subject are discussed thoroughly in Chapter 5. A few remaining items are covered here.

Arthritis

Arthritis means irritation of the joints. Most people who have this condition have pain in their joints and often difficulty moving them too. Even if you have arthritis, though, you should exercise regularly. If you don't use your joints, they will lose their function and you will find it difficult to move them at all. Exercise strengthens the muscles and ligaments surrounding a joint, making it more stable and less likely to be injured.

Cartilage is the white gristle that covers the ends of bones where they come together to form joints. People who have arthritis have cartilage that breaks easily. So people who have arthritis want to do enough exercise to strengthen their joints, but not so much exercise that it will break the cartilage in their joints.

The safest sports for people who have arthritis are swimming, cycling, and walking. When you swim, the buoyancy of the water acts as a cushion. When you ride a stationary bicycle, you remain seated, so that there is little force directly on your joints. When you walk, you always keep one foot on the ground, so that the force of your foot strike is rarely more than one times body weight. Jogging is very hard on your joints. During jogging, you have both feet off the ground at the same time, so that the force of your foot strike can be three times body weight.

Muscle Cramps

A cramp occurs when a muscle goes into spasm and stays that way. It can be caused by anything that interferes with the mechanisms that cause the muscle to contract or relax.

The brain sends a message along the nerves that lead to a muscle. When the signal from the nerves reaches the muscle, a chain of events governed by the movement of minerals inside and outside of the muscle cells causes the muscle to contract.

An electric current flows when there are different concentrations of minerals on opposite sides of a cell's membrane. In your body, each mineral has one or more electric charges. The sum of the charges from the minerals must be the same outside and inside the cells. If there is a difference in charge, electricity flows along the muscle.

Causes of Cramps

- Abnormal signals along nerves
- Abnormal concentrations of minerals inside or outside the cells
- An inadequate supply of oxygen
- An inadequate source of energy
- Damage to the muscle fibers
- Abnormal amounts of hormones or enzymes that govern muscle contractions

The minerals sodium and calcium are located primarily outside of the muscle cells, while potassium is located primarily inside of the cells. When the message from the brain reaches the muscle, calcium moves into the muscle cells and potassium moves out of the cells. This causes an electric current to flow along the muscle, which causes the muscle to contract. Then as the charges balance each other, the muscle relaxes.

For the muscle to contract and relax normally, it needs adequate supplies of fat and sugar to serve as energy sources and oxygen to help utilize these sources. It also needs the right concentrations of minerals inside and outside the cells.

Regardless of the cause, the treatment for cramps is the same. As shown in Chapter 4, you stretch the cramped muscle with one hand and squeeze and release the body of the muscle rhythmically with the other hand. For example, if you have a cramp in your calf, pull the front part of your foot up with one hand and squeeze the body of the calf muscle every few seconds.

Although the treatment for cramps does not depend on the cause, the prevention of cramps does depend on the cause. The timing of cramps can help you determine their source.

Cramps That Occur When You Start to Exercise

This problem is usually due to a mineral imbalance, such as a calcium deficiency, sodium deficiency, or potassium deficiency or excess. Abnormal blood levels of these minerals usually allow the muscle to contract but prevent it from relaxing. Blood tests will usually determine if you have abnormal mineral levels.

Cramps that occur when you start to exercise can also be due to low thyroid function or inability of the muscle to process sugar. Blood tests can be taken to measure thyroid function. A muscle biopsy must be taken to evaluate abnormal muscle metabolism.

Abnormal blood mineral levels are usually a sign that something is wrong with your body. A low potassium level usually is due to vomiting, taking diuretics, steroids or licorice, diarrhea, or a disease that affects your body's ability to take in and retain potassium. Magnesium deficiency is rare and is usually a sign of disease. If your doctor diagnoses that you lack magnesium, you need a complete and thorough evaluation to find out what is wrong in your body to cause this deficiency. Low or high blood levels of calcium are never normal. If your blood calcium level is abnormal, you probably have something wrong with your intestines, kidneys, or parathyroid glands, or you are poisoning yourself by taking in too much vitamin D.

Low salt (sodium) levels in your bloodstream are an extremely rare cause of muscle cramps. The American diet contains so much sodium that it is almost impossible to lose enough for you to become deficient. For example, your body needs 3,000 mgm of sodium when you exercise for many hours in very hot weather. If you were to stop salting your food and cooking with salt and didn't eat anything that tastes salty, you would still take in about 3,000 mgm of salt each day.

Cramps That Occur After You Exercise a Little

The most common cause is an inadequate blood supply to the muscle. At rest, your arteries may be large enough to transport the small amount of blood that your muscles require to function properly. However, when you exercise, your muscles require large amounts of oxygen-rich blood. If your arteries are not large enough to transport enough blood, your muscles will suffer from lack of oxygen and will go into spasm.

Cramps that occur soon after you start to exercise can also be due to abnormal mineral levels or rare diseases that interfere with your body's ability to utilize foodstuffs for energy. In that case, the diagnosis can be made only by having a surgeon cut out a small piece of muscle (a biopsy), so that it can be analyzed chemically.

Cramps That Occur After You Exercise For a Long Time

Dehydration is the most common cause. When you exercise for a long time, particularly in hot weather, you lose a lot of fluid. Your blood volume is reduced, and there may not be enough blood to supply oxygen to all your exercising muscles. As a result, the most actively exercising muscles may not get enough blood and they can go into spasm and hurt.

You can protect yourself from developing these kinds of cramps by drinking a cup of water before you exercise and at least every fifteen minutes while you exercise.

Cramps That Occur When You Sleep

Cramping during sleep is usually due to a pinched nerve or special muscle-tendon reflex. A nerve can be pinched when you turn in your sleep. This can cause a message to start at the site of the pinch and end up in the muscle. The muscle will contract in the same way as if the message had come from your brain.

Another cause is an exaggeration of a normal reflex in your body. When you turn during sleep, you contract your muscles. This stretches the attached tendons. There are certain nerve receptors in tendons which, when stretched, send a message back to your spinal cord. This causes a message to go back to the muscle, causing it to contract. Often it can stay contracted. When it does so, you develop a painful cramp. You can usually prevent night cramps by stretching before you go to bed the muscles that usually cramp.

Cramps That Occur Both at Rest and During Exercise

These cramps can be due to any of the above factors, but they are most frequently due to abnormal body levels of certain minerals, such as potassium, sodium, and calcium.

Stitches

A *stitch* is a cramp in the diaphragm, the large muscle that separates your chest from your abdomen and controls breathing. It is caused by a blockage of the blood supply to the diaphragm during exercise.

When you run, you lift your knees. This causes you to contract your belly muscles, so that the pressure inside your belly increases and presses on the diaphragm from below. During exercise, you may breathe hard and fast. Air gets *into* your lungs much more easily than it gets *out* of them. This causes the lungs to fill up with air and press on the diaphgram from above.

The dual pressure, from the lungs above and the belly muscles below, squeezes the diaphragm and shuts off the flow of blood to it. Any muscle that can't get enough oxygen will go into spasm and hurt.

If you develop a stitch, stop running. With your fingers, reach deeply into your belly just below your ribs on the right side. At the same time, purse your lips tightly and blow out as hard as you can. This should release the pressure on your diaphragm and you should be able to continue running painlessly.

AFTERWORD

We have attempted to give you all the information and inspiration you need to begin or continue a regular exercise program happily and painlessly. We hope we have succeeded in inspiring the non-exercisers among you to begin, the regular exercisers among you to continue and improve, and the scientists among you to help resolve the still-unanswered questions about sports medicine for women.

MONA SHANGOLD, M.D.
GABE MIRKIN, M.D.

INDEX